The Fallacy of Magnitude

A Collection of Writings

by Hugh J. Schonfield

The Fallacy of Magnitude
A Collection of Writings
by Hugh J. Schonfield

Edited by Stephen A. Engelking

Published by
Texianer Verlag
Tuningen Germany
www.texianer.com

on behalf of:

©2021 The Hugh & Helene Schonfield World Service
Trust

ISBN: 978394919796

Table of Contents

Preface

In rummaging through the archives of the Mondcivitan Republic, I came across a number of interesting essays and magazine articles that have never been published and written by Hugh Schonfield that I felt deserved to reach a wider audience.

Although the idea of founding a virtual Republic based on the concept of a serving world nation seems far-fetched to readers today, it expressed ideas of non-violence and sharing which perhaps will one day find themselves realised in another form from which their originator envisaged.

Hugh Schonfield arrived at his revelation of a Servant-People though his extensive research into Christian, Jewish and Biblical history. This becomes apparent when reading this collection of essays.

It has been a purpose of the Hugh and Helene Schonfield Trust to keep these ideas alive for that future generation who will one day take up the gauntlet of finding a way of creating a better and more peaceful world for all.

Schonfield's ideas did not fall on deaf ears and inspired many of his followers to make their own attempts of making this ancient dream a reality.

I have also included an essay from Sir Anthony Brooke who was a strong supporter of Schonfield's ideas.

It is hoped that the reader will find these essays both inspiring and a source of pleasure.

Stephen A. Engelking (Editor)

Short Biography of Hugh Schonfield

Hugh Joseph Schonfield was one of the most fascinating and amazing personalities of the 20th Century. He became a source of inspiration of the thinking of such celebrities as John Lennon. For some, the ideas he proposed were challenging and revealing, whilst others found them to be preposterous or even ridiculous. For certain groups they were even blasphemous and apparently worthy of death.

Apart from this obviously popular side to his work, it may be less known that he was also historian of the Suez Canal and was instrumental behind the scenes in a number of high level negotiations in the Middle East. So apart from being one of the most erudite historians of New Testament times, he was politically active in a most novel way. His official work in the Republic which he had caused to come to fruition would lead him to make proposals to governments, many of which would be integrated into final agreements. It has been suggested, for example, that his ideas played a role in the passing of the Test Ban Treaty.

He was a prodigious and skilled writer and researcher and was always on the look out for uncovering the truth and discovering novel interpretations.

It was these efforts and particularly his work for world peace which in fact caused him to be nominated for the Nobel Peace Prize. He fought inexhaustibly for this cause to his last dying breath, convinced that there was an eternal plan for a servant people (a "Dienstvolk" instead of a "Herrenvolk") to arise as the only lasting way of saving man from seemingly inevitable disaster..

He was also the first and only Jew to have translated the New Testament into English. I might add that this rendering is also one of the most informative, beautiful and understandable versions. (From "A Life for Mankind —The Biography of Hugh Joseph Schonfield")

The Fallacy of Magnitude

The famous Czech writer, Karel Capek, in his fantasy "War with the Newts," remarked on the human weakness for records and magnitude. A bad winter had to be the worst in living memory, a famine the severest ever known, a disaster the greatest and most tragic, a war the most destructive. Puny man is more readily stimulated by immensity. He feels challenged by the loftiest mountain, the possibility of reaching the greatest heights and the lowest depths. What is gigantic is more impressive and awe-inspiring than what is minute. To-day, we are being stirred by the existence of huge political power blocks, by the evidence of the enormous range and lethal potentialities of the hydrogen-bomb. We continue to respond to magnitude and react to immensity. We feel frustrated when we cannot make our opposition to these things of equal or greater bigness, rouse the masses, create a World Authority or World Government, establish an effective Third Camp. Even the non-violent want to negotiate from strength, from power, from might.

Yet the truth is that salvation does not lie in big battalions, in mass movements and monster demonstrations. Another writer of fantasies, H. G. Wells, imagined a "War of the Worlds" with an invasion of this planet by Mars. The Martians conquered the Earth with their immensely superior weapons and gigantic machines. "But," says the author, "there are no bacteria on Mars, and directly these invaders arrived, directly they drank and fed, our microscopic allies began to work their overthrow." In the end the Martians succumbed and were slain after all man's devices had failed, by the humblest things that God, in his wisdom, has put upon this earth."

There is a lesson here to be learnt by all who seek a better world order. We are wrong when we think that this end will be attained by big and authoritative agencies, by overwhelming numerical strength. We have to face up to this fundamental fallacy of magnitude and resist the delusive attractions of size. The world will be saved by what is despised and rejected, by the small and the weak and insignificant. It is not an easy lesson to learn and goes against all our inclinations. But it is essential that all of us in our tiny Commonwealth of World Citizens should learn it, and refuse to be carried away by the appeal of mere dimensions and loud clamour. Our duty to mankind is quietly and steadily to build out of ourselves, within the warring world, a miniature of a worthier society free from friction, to honeycomb all lands with centres of sanity, to nourish and develop the nucleus of the New Humanity. Every other method and programme will fail. It is such as we whom neither governments nor movements take into consideration, who actually hold the key to all the Future.

The Kingdom in the Midst

There has been much contention concerning what Jesus meant when he said "The Kingdom of God is within you." It is claimed that a no less accurate rendering would be "The Kingdom of God is among you." The fact is that the saying may be taken either way, for the text literally states "The Kingdom of God is in your midst."

But why have people taken sides on this issue? Why does it matter so vitally? It is because some believe the Kingdom to be a subjective spiritual experience in the soul and others an objective spiritual order in the world. Surely both positions are true, and our understanding will be incomplete and our progress towards the Kingdom will be hindered unless we can recognise and reconcile them in one body individually and collectively. Neither attitude is wholly true and sufficient in itself.

The Holy Servant Nation expresses for us the means by which the Kingdom of God is to be realised; and so inevitably this issue comes again to the fore, and there are those who see the process psychologically and those who see it politically. The one suggests that we must personally be changed before we can create a new order, and the other that we must create a new order to provide the conditions for personal change.

There is no escape from the dilemma posited by these opposing viewpoints except by reconciling them. They have to be apprehended as two parts of one whole, and not tolerated merely, but incorporated in each individual and in the group. And the only agency that can bring this about is the universal cohesive power of Love.

Otherwise despair and futility supervene, and the bright vision of the Kingdom in the Midst becomes an intangible and evermore elusive Kingdom in the Mist.

Breaking Through

It was H. G. Wells, in one of his earlier fantasies, The Wonderful Visit, who explained that the heavenly sphere and the earthly sphere were not separate and distinct places but co-occupants of precisely the same space on a different plane of consciousness. Heaven was in fact on the earth all the time and as material and substantial a world as that in which we live and move and have our being. The two interpenetrated and under certain conditions there could be a "break through" of men into heaven and of angels into the earth.

We catch something of the same idea in seeing pictures of a particular place as it looked fifty or even two hundred years ago, and as it appears to-day. The space, the area, is the same; but it wears an entirely different aspect: it is another world, another age, another life. The cine-camera captures for us a similar effect by its instantaneous dissolution of the one scene into the other across the gulf of centuries. Artificially we have been permitted to "break through" in Time. To some, however, such an achievement may come without a scientific illusion or mechanical aid, as in An Adventure, the account of the strange experience of the two ladies walking in the Gardens of Versailles who suddenly found themselves in the same gardens in the days of Marie Antoinette. They had somehow, and with no sense of transition, moved in Time but not in Space.

These considerations, and others to which they give rise, may help us with our problem and forward us upon the path of reconciliation. The Kingdom of God is described in one place as "the days of heaven upon the earth." Heaven has "broken through" : the City of God has "come down." But the Kingdom, unrealised by the many, always was "in the midst," it always was both in us and among us, but denied manifestation.

Thus we can realise the Holy Nation as a translation of a normally invisible reality into a visible reality, its "breaking through" from spiritual and philosophical apprehension into social and political constitution. It is another order of nationhood co-extensive with the materially existing world of nations, interpenetrating and impinging upon it, and "breaking through" into it and activating it.

By in it we begin to understand how the truth that "our citizenship is in heaven" becomes manifested in actual world citizenship, how we can be in this world and yet not of it, how geography is for us no handicap, frontiers no barrier, how our society can function within any society, and our ministry become effective among men.

The Dinosaurs

A great deal has been written about the laws of Natural Selection, and in one particular they certainly do embody a principle which has an important bearing on the Service-Nation Movement and the present crisis of civilisation.

Far back in the days of the primeval monsters we have a first glimpse of this principle in operation on our planet. We see how a concentration on self- defence, the creation of barriers, hardening and crystalisation is a sure sign that the Life Force has spent itself. With the dinosaurs and the other gigantic lizards of the Mesozoic this stage had been reached. The brain became puny: they were encased in armour plate: they lost fluidity, mobility, and expansiveness; and so for them life had ended. The future lay with the insignificant, unprotected, unregarded creatures, ancestors of the mammals, nimble, mobile, mentally alert and sensitive. As Gerald Heard has written of a later stage: "Once again the real Natural Selection, the test of feeling and awareness had to be applied. Once again choice had to be made of a creature who as yet enjoyed nothing, had carved out for itself no kingdom, who was master and authority in no sphere." (The Source of Civilisation.)

Heard goes on to show how the principle has continually applied. "As among all animals, as again among all mammals when at last they dominated, so now when man of all animals and of all mammals alone dominates, the same process of selection is at work among his races and stocks. The vast majority, we must expect, will specialise, play for safety and security, defend themselves—even more than against their fellows—against the intolerable strain of persisting in sensitiveness, in awareness, in sympathy and understanding. They will shut down, and from being defensive become offensive and finally parasitic and so extinct. One strain will find the more excellent way and seeming to be set on losing its life will alone gain it."

We can see the principle exemplified in all the historic crises of mankind. The Hebrew prophet visioned the old imperialisms as dinosauric monsters, hard and vindictive, cruel and insensitive, destined inevitably to pass away, and their place to be taken by the unprotected, mobile and feeling "people of the saints of the Most High" (Book of Daniel). The armour-plated might of ancient Rome, symbolised by the legions, and barren of creative thought, represented such a monster. "In every sense of the term," says Professor Whitehead, "the Western Empire had lacked expansive force. Across the Rhine and the Danube the northern forests were impenetrable. On the west, the Atlantic Ocean was trackless. With the minor exception of the conquest of Britain, all attempt at physical expansion ceased after Varus lost the legions of Augustus. The Western Empire in all its ramifications was a purely defensive institution, in its sociological functionings and in its external behaviour. Its learning lacked speculative adventure. In no sense, however we stretch the metaphor, did it discover a "New World" (Adventures of Ideas). Life, he states, demands expansion and novelty; and so Rome was ready to pass away. The future belonged to the despised, weak and unprotected new nation of Christians, sensitive, fluid and mobile, uniting the spiritual dynamic of the Hebrews with the speculative inquisitiveness of the Greeks.

The same hardening, crystalising process, however, was to overtake the Church when it made the grievous error of assuming the mantle of Rome. In turn it became armour-plated, insensitive, and incapable of expansion, another dinosaur. Clamping down on scientific enquiry the Church could force a Galileo to recant on his knees; but it could not prevent his murmuring of their static earth: "It does move, just the same." So the Church of that time had to give way before the spirit of free thought and mobility of ideas.

Always it has been the same. Natural Selection preferred the unprotected serfs to the robber barons in their castle strongholds : the nimble bowman with their long-ranging arrows won the victory in the field over the armoured knights. The static is forever overcome by the dynamic. The wind and the rain and the flowing water will wear down the most invincible rock. Security and solidity spell death. Life is with the free, with those who are "born of the spirit."

Once again to-day the eternal laws write with unerring finger the judgment upon our civilisation: "Weighed in the balance, and found wanting." Sentence of death is pronounced on the dinosaurs. Our armour-plated age, with its accent on defence, impregnability, and security, rejecting sensitiveness and sympathy, is doomed. Whatever is defensive, whatever seeks self-sufficiency, whatever is harsh and intolerant, which raises barriers whether material or abstract, is ripe for extinction. The future is not with the frontier-bound states : it is with the fluid, unprotected agencies.

Let us not then be troubled that the Service-Nation Movement is condemned as impossibly idealistic by those obsessed by the apparent power of mass organisation. Let us bear cheerfully that our weakness is despised, our mobility of thought is scorned, and our purpose to create a free nation of world citizens is contrasted unfavourably with a collective security programme. We the unprotected, the servants of all, are the true pioneers of the New World. With us rests the hope of mankind.

"The Lord saveth not with sword and spear." That is the eternal lesson of the story of the armour-plated giant Goliath and the unprotected shepherd boy David. The lesson is the same as that of the primeval dinosaurs and the little lithe, shy creatures to whom they were forced to yield. "Oh, little guy, what if to-day your knees do quake and your heart beats faster as you walk in the presence of the monsters of power. Be of good cheer, little guy! You

have licked the giants before." (W.A. Allen, The Rotarian,
July 1943.)
      "Blessed are the meek: for they shall inherit the earth."

Race, Class and Creed

The great conflicts which afflict mankind today derive substantially from the clash between slower-moving and faster-moving elements under conditions which demand a very rapid acceleration in the processes of change and adjustment. From a variety of causes the vast majority of the Earth's population is severely handicapped in making the unprecedented response that is called for.

1. Race

The planet man occupies is zoned, with belts of cold, temperate, sub-tropical and torrid regions, which have changed only to a relatively minor extent over thousands of years. These regions not only have a physical configuration in the shaping of land and water areas: the land masses themselves differ considerably in features such as mountains and rivers, deserts and fertile territories, and in what they offer specifically of natural resources both to support life and to determine its character and quality.

On the whole, and allowing for various migrations and invasions, there has been a prolonged experience of adaptation to geographical environment, which has had an impact on ethnical characteristics and cultures. Much of this has been very long-term; but in modern times it has been possible to see the emergence in a very brief period of new types such as the white Australian and the negro American.

One should not therefore speak of inferior and superior races as regards potential capacity, but of peoples whose situations and circumstances have produced differences in pigmentation, disposition, and mode of existence. Where scientific and technological progress has been most prominent has chiefly been in the more temperate regions, where also in the confrontation of a number of ethnical groups within a restricted space the pressures of living have been greater. Primitive societies in other regions have not been under the same necessity to change their ways.

Other factors have been influential, such as in some zones the prolific increase in population and in isolated neighbourhoods the consequences of inbreeding.

What we are adducing does not pass judgment in the respective worth of cultures and civilizations. It simply illustrates that for survival the processes of change have had to be speeded-up much more in some parts of the world than in others, thus bringing about distinctions of outlook, equipment and behaviour patterns, and producing a diversity of life-styles.

There is an important evolutionary value in this diversification, because its variety and colourfulness prevents inertia and acts as an incentive to development.

Many of the disparities are now being broken down, though as yet mainly on the surface. Partly this has been due to colonial expansion over the past five hundred years, especially of European states. The aim was to increase wealth and prosperity, and latterly to gain access to and exploit those materials demanded in ever greater quantity and type by the advancements of science and technology. Today the chief industrialised societies are still located in the temperate zone belts of the upper and lower hemispheres, particularly the upper with its much more extensive land mass. Consequently it is the countries in these belts, notably the more powerful ones, which tend to be economically 'imperialistic' no matter what may be their political complexion.

Another cause has been the recent unprecedented advance in the means and speed of transport and communication, while a third has been the conquest of environment by technology which has permitted temperate zone conditions to be reproduced in other zones, together with the engineering skills and medical knowledge to bring such zones forward in the provision of means of subsistence and expectation of life.

The intrusion of temperate zone life-styles into the other zones where the tempo of development had been slower has had its effects in disturbing the rhythm, causing psychological distress, racial disharmony, an artificial imitation of alien political and social structures, and a sense of resentment against exploitation.

At no previous period have the different life-styles of the world come into such close contact and relationship. The juxtaposition in work and community has served to put a new emphasis on race and contributed to fostering ethnical antagonism.

Especially has the universalization of the nation-state structure, together with substantial population increases in many countries, helped to promote prejudice against aliens. While some enlightened efforts are being made both nationally and internationally to tackle this problem they have as yet had no great success; and it is to be feared that ethnic hostility will increase, particularly if economic conditions should seriously deteriorate. It will take a long time to achieve some approximation to equality of status, opportunity and respect for human rights. We have to note the tendency to create alliances and blocs on racial lines.

On the beneficial side, however, the evidence of a two-way traffic is not to be disregarded. Just as the impact of the temperate zones is forcing upon the others a phenomenal acceleration of change, so the less restless, stoical and contemplative attitudes of tropical regions is contributing somewhat to modifying and toning down the urge to unrelenting activity evinced by temperate zone peoples. Already there has been some imparting of a sense of values which pertain to a quieter, more spiritual and life-concerning concept of evolutionary development.

A greater equilibrium will eventually result when the nation-state has been outgrown and international organs of government have become operative. Until this happens it is vain to speak of mankind as a unity, and we have to accept that the vast majority of all races because of their depressed circumstances cannot be expected to be responsive at this stage to an inter-racial stimulus.

Accordingly, it devolves upon a sentient minority to engage in an over-all planning for harmony. It is an undertaking which calls for the emergence of a new species, the planetary or world man, who is the expression of a multi-racial identity, and whose commitment to serving all mankind makes no distinctions.

The Mondcivitan Republic is the vehicle of this evolutionary development, drawing its citizens from all climes and races and welding them together in a world-distributed Servant-Nation restricted by no frontiers or divisions. It is creating in the process the working-model of a united world, and advancing its advent by the inspiration of its example and activities.

2. Class

The effects of differentiation between the slow-moving and faster-moving components of mankind do not only arise from climatic and geographical causes. They derive also from the class structures of the world's populations.

Class stratification was the almost inevitable consequence of civilization, using that term in its exact sense. To a limited extent it existed already in primitive societies. But with the much more elaborate organization represented by the city-state and its controlled territories there was demanded a greater diversification of function.

It was no accident that one of the early engineering feats was the construction of the pyramid ziggurat, broad at the base and narrowing to a point at the top. Apart from representing an observed form of natural stability, the hill or mountain, it no less symbolized a stabilized ordering of human existence. At the bottom was the bulk of the population with the addition of slaves serving as a poor and depressed labour force, while at the top was the patron deity exercising his or her delegated authority and protection through a government vested in a priesthood and court. The intermediate functional layers were occupied by the skilled artisans, the traders and merchants, and the supervisors, stewards and executive officials.

The system engendered a gradation of condition and competency. The majority lived in squalor and without education except in methods of production, while wealth, amenities and culture increased from level to level in a narrowing ascending application. Only exceptionally could the individual improve his station through determination, natural ability and strength of character. Not until in more advanced societies education progressively reached down over many centuries to offer culture and mental development to the lower orders could the pattern slowly change and the responsive move up the scale according to inclination and equipment, and even if so desired occupy the seats of government.

This is a brief and generalized presentation, since civilizations have not been identical either contemporaneously or from age to age. Factors like the growth of trade could unite the merchant with the baronial aristocracy, and bring pressure to bear on governments to reduce their autocratic powers. Representation of the people could develop in more democratic societies. Industrialization could give rise to a new governing class. The increase of armed forces could make possible the institution of military dictatorships.

But it is broadly correct to convey that the pyramidal structure has hitherto prevailed, and that consequently the majority of the world's population has remained handicapped and retarded, and therefore has been much more slow-moving in the growth of consciousness and the range of comprehension which comes from the stimulus of learning and the exercise of imagination.

Popular education, so far as it has gone, has however been bringing about important changes. In the first place it has enabled the labouring masses to become aware that their essential contribution to the state economy gave them the power greatly to improve their circumstances. Through the formation of Trades Unions they could bargain effectively with employers and make demands on governments. They could even organise politically to gain control of governments Here the objective was the elimination of a privileged class and the utilization of national resources for the benefit of the working class. This has been described as the class war or class struggle.

On the whole, by reason of its sense of grievance, the so-called proletariat has been most tenacious of a class consciousness, so that it has been the category of society least able to adjust to the idea of the replacement of class by a structure which permitted full freedom to the individual. The goal has been much more a one class society than a classless one. Socialism cannot tolerate private enterprise because it associates it with exploitation for personal gain, which is still a feature of free societies. But underlying this intolerance is the design to prevent anyone getting out of step with his fellows and obtaining the liberty of independence of control. A socialist society has to be fault-finding, bureaucratically watchful and continually on guard against deviation. Being restrictive and mistrustful it cannot be happy and at ease.

Since the old privileged class, privileged in the sense of ruling by virtue of right and place in the social scheme, has largely now disappeared, the workers have tended to distinguish as a class all who have a measure of independence and freedom of choice by reason of some kind of ownership and private means. This stratum of society does not however have the rigidity of a class, and those who belong to it are frequently of working-class origin.

What is exhibited by the upper levels of society today is a growing emancipation from class-consciousness and a greater regard for individuality. The emphasis is on personal qualities, character, gifts and attainments. There is a liberty to be more Liberal and progressive, and a capacity to be concerned with others on a basis of genuine concern and humanitarianism.

Viewpoints are able to be more comprehensive and universal.

They can of course alternatively be more selfish and self-seeking.

There is thus a division of the world on lines of individualism versus collectivism. Both have merits and demerits.

The Mondcivitan position is that the two do not have to be in opposition. The clash arises from power motivation, the to dominate and control for secctional and selfish ends. Mondcivitans stress that the Good Society has to be motivated by the principle of Service, mutual well-being and cooperation being the objective instead of power-seeking.

The principle of service acknowledges the entitlement of the individual to full self-development according to capacity, but in association with the acceptance of obligations and the discharge of responsibilities towards the community as a whole. The level of potentiality to enjoy a full life has continually to be raised, and the worth of the individual is not to be judged by the nature of the task performed. Where fellowship prevails class ceases to be relevant.

By reason of its character and purpose the Mondcivitan Republic is in a unique position to demonstrate the qualities of the New Society in its own structure.

3. Creed

Religion in the past has been another fruitful cause of war, cruelty and oppression. The integration of distinct societies whether tribal or political was assisted by the acceptance of a patron deity, who by supernatural power could supplement human effort by control of the elements and the resources on which life depended, and by lending superior strength to his or her adherents. The deity was suitably to be propitiated to secure favours, and could inflict dire punishment for neglect and apostasy.

In internal relations Religion therefore served as the cement which bonded the social layers together and gave coherence to the whole, while externally it inspired resistance to aggression and authorised foreign conquest. In war the shrines and images of the enemy's deities were the particular objects of destruction or capture and the religion of the conquerors was often imposed on the defeated, while in peace visiting members of other peoples would think it well or politic to pay their respects and make offerings to the deity of the locality.

Ethnically and in a class context Religion operated conservatively as the maintainer of a fixed order and the repository of tradition. At the same time it helped both individuals and the masses to bear their sufferings, and in more enlightened societies it acted as a restraining influence on evildoing and injustice.

In general Religions tended to vary in character and expression according to climatic and physical conditions and degrees of civilization. Their distinguishing features might be attributed to special inspirations, but largely they represented the qualities of different life-styles.

We are here considering dogmatic Religion expressed in creed, which emphasized superiority and demanded conformity, and which consequently lent itself to intolerance and persecution.

Religion of course has another side, associated with spiritual awareness and aspiration, contributing to moral growth and benevolence, and a deeper understanding of the meaning and purpose of life. The existence and activity of transcendental Being is a perception of spiritual consciousness which has followed its own path of evolution with a refining and elevating effect. Religions have given an impetus to spiritual development, but their institutional structure and involvements could not keep pace with it.

Further on the credit side of Religion has been the urge towards higher self-fulfilment, not only for the individual but for the collectivity of mankind. The latter could envisage a Golden Age of peace and happiness as the end-product of creation, and in this sense of a plan it was the prophet rather than the priest whose vision and influence was chiefly in evidence. Frequently the two were in collision. The prophets have been much more alive to the need for social change and much less attached to religious institutions and dogmas. As a consequence they have often suffered at the hands of the secular religious authorities.

Under the impact of modern reasoning and scientific discovery, and also in many parts of the world the divorcement of Faiths from alliance with States, there has been a tendency for priesthoods to move over to the side of the prophets. But this trend is still hampered by dogmatism and the assertion of sacerdotal authority.

With greater awareness of man's capacities and problems, and progress in education, a new division is increasingly manifesting itself. On the one hand there is a greater individualism with people determining for themselves what they will believe, forming their own personal convictions. These may represent any kind of combination or interpretation of the traditional Faiths, or they may be identified with some form of Humanism, whether Agnostic or Atheistic.

On the other hand there is reversion to collectivism, drawing upon both racial and class consciousnesses. Here the old Religions have been replaced by Ideologies; but they exhibit a similar credal dogmatism and consequently a persecuting intolerance. The most prominent are Fascism or Nazism, and additionally Black Power, which have a racial emphasis, and Communism, whether Marxist-Leninist or Trotskyite, which is inspired by a working class Socialism. Where the Ideologies are associated with States there is not much to choose between them as regards ruthlessness and bigotry.

Modern ideological conflict and repression of individual freedom has in fact brought back the worse features of the old religious systems and is destructive of the hard won concept of the Rights of Man.

Citizens of the Mondcivitan Republic enjoy complete freedom of conscience. But they aim to create not merely a Free Society but a Good Society, one which promotes a sense of communal responsibility on the basis of a caring fellowship. Power motivation is replaced by a Service motivation. And this is operative externally as well as internally, as laid down in the Seven Principles of the Republic embodied in its Constitution.

Consequently Mondcivitans go further than the Declaration of Human Rights, and seek to bring out and make operative the best in human nature in all the relationships of mankind.

In this Paper it is recognized that deep-seated emotions, not in themselves unworthy, are aroused by Race, Class and Creed. Partly these reflect protective and herd instincts, which in Man by reason of his development and greater acquisitiveness have stimulated aggressiveness. The pursuit of power has played on these emotions to create hostility and conflict. But there has also manifested itself in Man a corrective spirit of altruistic humanitarianism and disinterested service, and it is in promoting and exemplifying this that division can be converted into harmony. Diversity then becomes a cause of mutual attraction and inspiration.

This essay was intended by Hugh Schonfield as an introduction to as series of study and discussion papers entitled "The Mondcivitan World View". Its author composed the following introduction to the series:

This series of Papers has been prepared for the Department of Education of the Mondcivitan Republic and is designed both for individual citizens and groups.

The Papers aim to promote a world attitude to world issues, and to stimulate thought on the contribution of the Republic as the Servant-Nation of mankind. The Mondcivitan task is both a positive and peculiar one, and calls therefore for an equipment of understanding and impartiality which will enable our people to express themselves clearly to others and apply creative imagination to the structure and activities of the Republic.

A limited number of themes has been selected, and they are not treated in great detail, so that there is ample scope to develop the subjects and to pursue others to which they give rise. It is hoped to evoke both questions and practical proposals; but these should not be hastily formulated. What is vital is to absorb and digest ideas in order to acquire a Mondcivitan outlook.

That outlook has to be honest and objective, and inspired by the desire to aid and serve. Not to be critical would be wholly unrealistic. We have to cultivate a capacity for discernment, but at the same time judgment has to be free from bias and malice. None of us is wholly immune to the prevailing tensions, and we have to be on our guard that they are not influencing us in our interpretations. The Mondcivitan has to be involved without being partisan, and analytical without prejudice. We are building a new comprehensive approach to the world and its problems which takes account of the past and reaches constructively forward into the future. We are identified with a specific Plan the character of which we have both to exemplify and bring progressively into remedial operation for the benefit and unification of humanity.

The Servant Nation in Modern Times

Since the end of the 19th century there has been a growing awareness that Mankind needs some sort of representation if peace is to come upon the Earth.

There were many brave attempts to achieve this, mostly based on the notion that a league of nations would be able to negotiate and mediate at times of conflict. Prior to the Second World War, due to the work and vision of the Jewish scholar, Hugh Schonfield, a revival of the notion of a holy or servant nation based on Biblical prophecy and the universal Hope gained increasing sympathy, particularly in England.

A 'Movement for a Holy Servant Nation' was established with a view to constituting a nation in diaspora which would be universalist in its appeal and Messianic at its foundation. It would be beyond religion, oriented towards impartiality and work for peace. Its people would have a clear set of principles based on the fundamental Law.

In 1952, The Mondcivitan Republic or Commonwealth of World Citizens, was formally constituted as a Servant Nation. It gained some recognition and held international elections and parliament. It was able to mediate in some instances and gained an increasing number of citizens with its headquarters in central London. The International Arbitration League founded by Sir William Randall Cremer at the end of the 19th Century was incorporated into it giving it a tradition now of over 100 years.

However, the Republic as such faded away and it ceased to have an office or official base. The Constitution which had been so bravely created was suspended and the responsibility for the Republic's affairs and archives were put into the hands of the Hugh and Helene Schonfield World Service Trust. Why the Republic failed is a matter of conjecture but it is certain that both society and the thinking of individuals have changed so much that its manner of organization would not be appropriate in today's world.

It became increasingly clear that a new approach was called for. Patience is a great teacher and we have had to wait this long before new personalities with new ideas could appear which would make a new interpretation feasible. It became increasingly obvious that a revival which insisted on the old form of the Mondcivitan Republic would not find the attention which it received at its former constitution in 1952. Such a concept would be unlikely to be understood as effective in today's political landscape.

Additionally, it became more and more obvious that without finding a common base of understanding between those coming from the various cultures emanating from the Jewish, Christian and Islamic cultures, the aspirations of world peace were unlikely to find a realization. Somehow, the way ahead seemed to be embodied in a new understanding of the Messianic, of a renewed Israel not bound to territory or religion. This new Israel would be inclusive, peace-loving and oriented on the Messianic. It would open its arms to all who would embrace its principles based on the eternal concept of Love. It was decided to retain the original Mondcivitan Principles and to encourage not only a corporate but lived-out personal interpretation of these.

We would not be inviting people to a new religion but rather to an acknowledgement of the eternal hope for mankind's peace and happiness and to share this in the form of exemplary nationhood. A new people for a new world. Any change in society would have to start with us individuals. The person of Jesus the Nazorean would be an example to us of Servant Leadership yet we would refuse to worship him as a god but see him as an example of the Messianic interpretation—'the first of many brethren'. We would rediscover and take up that discipleship and commitment and continue the work of building a nation set apart for the service of mankind.

Those of us who felt strongly that the world's salvation could only happen through a servant people based on the ancient calling preserved in some form in all noble religions and philosophical ideas started to form a a community–an Israel or Servant Nation in diaspora—of those who wished to make the idea a reality. We have started to try and form a new expression and draw others into the circle. Our greatest hope is that you will now join us.

I Will Build Again

Brooding upon the problems of the world today, it is easy to give way to despair; for what has man not tried in his earnest efforts to rear up a stable and permanent international structure? Always the result has been failure in greater or lesser degree. The more imposing the edifice, the more fearful has been its fall.

Yes, there are constructive policies that have not been tried, sounder, it is said, bolder, more ambitious, and we are invited to test them as the sole alternative to perishing miserably. But how, living amidst the disintegrating fragments of past schemes, shall we place any credence in them? Will not they also come toppling down in ghastly confusion? If we are honest with ourselves we shall admit that neither Metropolis nor Cosmopolis, nor other high-sounding name for the architecture of a new order, carries with it any real and abiding conviction. We see too clearly that each of these projects assumes that the weight of its towering superstructure can be carried on the flimsiest of supporting columns. Where, we ask, are the pillars of love, goodwill and self-sacrifice to bear this mass? And there is no answer.

We can afford to take no more leaps in the dark. We cannot allow ourselves to be deluded into imagining that the first conditions of security can be so recklessly disregarded. Better to give up striving than to live in a fool's paradise that seems to satisfy so many of our reputed wise men.

The Neglected Plan of God

When we have turned away in discerning rejection from the clamour of scheme hucksters, we may be prepared to give heed to the Plan of God lying neglected—like the book of the Law in the temple in King Josiah's time—in the foundations beneath the crumbling heaps of our spiritual and cultural sanctuary. Reading the message with awe and repentance, we also may cry: "Go ye, enquire of the Lord for me, and for the people, and for all Israel, concerning the words of the book that is found: for great is the wrath of the Lord that is kindled against us, because our fathers have not hearkened unto the words of this book to do according unto all that which is written concerning us."

Our situation will immediately appear in a new light, a prophetic light, and we shall see distinctly why all our contrivances have come to nothing, and why we have arrived at our present predicament. Revelation will show us where we have erred, and how we must set about constructing a society "builded compactly together," a holy society, a City of God that will endure. And with revelation will come courage and vision, for now we are inspired by the Architect of the Universe, and nothing is overlooked in His design.

Once we have recovered the Plan of God there is nothing to hinder us from going forward with the work. We must begin first to clear away the rubbish down to the foundations. Let us spare no tears or sentiment for the accumulations of time-honoured traditions, or seek to preserve the vestiges of what we have become accustomed to regard as our precious inheritance. Our business is not to salvage civilisation, but to get down to bedrock and start again. We shall frequently be surprised and regretful at what we have to discard, but often glad to find stones left whole that can be used again.

The Earth's Most Ancient Enmity

If these things are in the nature of a parable, they will soon be interpreted realistically enough.

Already it is possible to clarify some of the issues. How is it to be supposed that the contemporary jealousies between nations are capable of being banished so long as the oldest international enmity in the world continues?

How can there be the remotest prospect of peace on earth until envy and hatred between Jew and Gentile has ceased? These questions are fundamental. Revelation discovers for us that the Jews and the Christians are called to be the fellow-builders of the Kingdom of God. The destiny of the one is bound up with the other. Together they represent the olive tree of Israel (Rom. xii). United they constitute a "kingdom of priests and a holy nation." They are the nation which God has ordained as the mediator and arbitrator among the nations, the supra-territorial, disinterested and impartial authority for which all sincere political theorists have been questing in vain. He has planned that like should be served by like, a God-instructed nation to serve the nations. No Hague Court, League or Federalism, or Commission of Neutrals can do perfect justice as the holy people can do it.

This truth carries with it a heavy responsibility on which Christians are now called to meditate and pray. The jews will have to return to their messianic mission through a spiritual revival; but they at least are known as an international people, representative of every country and class, and yet distinct. But Christians, though they believe in a Church universal and are in a sense a world community, have not for centuries considered themselves as members of a nation. Revelation, however, plainly states that they are a nation, an integral part of the people of Israel. "Ye are a chosen generation, a royal priesthood, an holy nation, a peculiar people; that ye should shew forth the praises of Him Who hath called you out of darkness into His marvellous light: which in time past were not a people, but are now the people of God" (1 Peter ii., 9-10). The teaching of St. Paul is the same. "Wherefore remember, that ye being in time past Gentiles... that at that time ye were without Christ, being aliens from the commonwealth of Israel... but now in Christ Jesus ye who sometimes were far off are made nigh by the blood of Christ. For He is our peace, Who hath made both (Jew and non-Jew) one, and hath broken down the middle wall of partition between us" (Eph. ii., 11.13). The promise was made to Abraham that in his seed should all the nations of the earth be blessed, and St. Paul tells the former Gentiles: "If ye be Christ's, then are ye Abraham's seed, and heirs according to the promise" (Gal. iii,, 29).

I Will Build Again the Tabernacle of David

The Plan of God is that a holy nation consisting of the Jews with the "called out" from among the Gentiles "shall judge among the nations, and shall rebuke many peoples: and they shall beat their swords into plough-shares, and their spears into pruning hooks: nation shall not lift up sword against nation, neither shall they learn war any more" (Isa. ii., 4). There will be no peace in the world until that nation is functioning as a nation. This is the only practical solution to our international problems, and this is the message we are called upon to proclaim to-day.

The time is coming when Jews and Christians will be required to surrender their present nationality and legally to take upon themselves nationality in the name of Israel, the name of divine service for all mankind. There will then be no question of divided loyalty.

It was in the light of this knowledge that the President of the first Christian National Council could say: "To this agree the words of the prophets; as it is written, After this I will return, and will build again the tabernacle of David, which is fallen down; and I will build again the ruins thereof; and I will set it up: that the residue of men might seek after the Lord, and all the Gentiles, upon whom My name is called, saith the Lord, who doeth all these things. Known unto God are all His works from the beginning of the world" (Acts xv,, 15-17).

*from an article in The Christian Pacifist New Series.
No. 5. Vol. 2 May 1940.*

Whence and Whither

At one time I was so deeply impressed with the wording of the first chapter of Genesis that I undertook an experiment which would take account of the primitive significance of the words employed, the ideas they represented. For in essence words were pictograms. So in the three- lettered root of every Hebrew word there was a hidden image illustrative of the thoughts and activities of primitive humanity. By comparing the employment of these roots one could largely arrive at the basic ideas behind them. I was anxious to see how the opening verses of Genesis would come out if subjected to this kind of analysis. The results were quite surprising, and I presented them in an article published in a long-defunct magazine called *The Quest*. One could feel that one was sitting at the feet of the Matriarch, who in the cloudy days of infant humanity was telling her tribal children the story of how the world began.

There was even an emphatic play on sound in the telling, which the English Bible has failed to reproduce. I refer to the words (Gen. i. 2) that the Earth "was without form and void" which in Hebrew is tohu wavohu. I thought to reflect both sense and sound by the rendering:

"Now the Earth was featureless and creatureless."

The interpretation of Genesis is not my theme. But I have wanted to represent something of the awareness in the opening verses of the Bible of a mystery behind the visible universe, the mystery of a very positive but undisclosed intention, which made it essential to bring Man on the scene. The world was being made ready for what would take place upon its surface, like a stage set for a drama. At least this was how the Hebrews peculiarly saw it.

I reproduce here the effect of my investigation as applying to the Bible's first five verses, while retaining some of the language with which we are familiar.

First of all God created the Sky and the Earth.
Now the Earth was featureless and creatureless, and
a stillness was upon the surface of the deep.
Only the Wind of God ruffled the surface of the wa-
ters.
And God said, 'Let there be a stirring! '
And a stirring took place.
And God regarded the stirring with approval.
And God distinguished stirring-time from still-time.
Stirring-time He called Day, and still-time He called
Night.
Thus passive and active was One Day.

We live in an age of coal and oil. We employ the mineral and other resources of our planet for our structures, our machines, our economics, and our medicaments. But what has provided these essentials of our advanced society? They have largely been the residual products of the organic and inorganic life billions of years before the coming of Man. We could not have what we are pleased to call our civilization. We could not progress in the complexities and potentialities of our Way of Life. We could not now be beginning to penetrate and explore our solar system, were it not for all that was stored away in remote antiquity, when there was no indication that such a thing as a human being would ever exist.

We can go still further back now, and. marvel at the conjunction of circumstances which made our puny planet within our solar system peculiarly fitted to harbour and develop life.

It does not appear particularly appropriate to ascribe these circumstances to chance. In the context of the designs of which we are capable they give evidence of intention. And, of course, if there was intention there was an objective which a remote future would in due course disclose. If, them, our planet, and life upon it in an ascending scale, was not accidental, this suggests that not only was Man created for a purpose, but that in the story of Man all history is at least to an extent purposeful. And its objectives could not be reached without the provisions and conjunctions of circumstances which would become operative at stages along the way.

Let us not be too critical of how the Bible opens. There is a primitive discernment in it, which may be more discerning than the concentrations of science on the analysis of primeval progress. Fundamentally it ascribes to Powers-that-be (plural form *Elohim*, a purpose in creation which called for preparatory organization and rhythm conducive to the manifestation and perpetuation of a life-cycle, governed by recuperative periods and the intake of sustenance. It was first of all the structure of the whole business, the way in which everything seemed to have been anticipated and provided for, that awed the Hebrew mind. And. when this turned to Man, the crown of creation, there was the recognition that homo sapiens had the edge of all living creatures in that he could more positively reason and imagine, and devise artefacts for the improvement of his circumstances. Unlike many peoples who saw God in the forces of nature, the luminaries, and alien living-creatures, the Hebrews saw Man as the Son of God, since to a degree he shared the capacities and constructive initiatives of the Creator of the Universe. It could be deduced that for Man's service as Son of God all things visible and invisible had been devised.

But since Man was a created being he could not himself be God. He was subject to change and decay. He was not perfect as God is perfect. He had to be educated for whatever his function was intended to be. This involved experience and experiment, trial, testing and judgement-forming. The Bible describes Man's first failure as arising from his humanity. He was capable of yielding to temptation, of coming to wrong conclusions, of being deceived.

For whatever high purpose Man was intended, he could not embark upon it until its first requirements had registered by deprivation of the notable attributes of his exalted status. One of these was immortality. The Bible assigns the Fall to the female element in Man's nature, springing from his earthiness. Man had come from God, but woman had come from man. Thus Man was brought down from his pedestal, so that he might learn humility. Driven from Paradise, and involved henceforth as a mortal in all the pains and perils of his humanity, Man must climb back the hard way to capacity to act and work for God, motivated by the retained attributes of the Divine in him. He had to face that he was a hybrid, half animal, half angel.

This consciousness, the Bible indicates, was not universally present in the world. It was transmitted through those descendants of Adam who would receive at least a partial revelation of God's purpose in creating Man. By emphasising *The Book of the Generations of Adam* (*Gen.* v. 1) the Bible repudiates that its theme is Theology. It represents itself rather as a revelation of God's anthropology.

Thus the Hebrew concepts were not pantheistic, deifying in appropriate images Divine attributes and natural forces, or the phenomena of the skies. Equally they did not seek to define God in the Hellenic manner of the Christian creeds, Nicene and Athanasian. For the Hebrews God's nature was indescribable and indepictable. It could only be said of Him, "I am what I am." This was a very remarkable achievement of the Hebrew perception. It assigned to God a realm of Being where Man as Man did not function. As the Bible put it: "Heaven, even the heavens, are the Lord's; but the earth hath He given to the Children of Men." in this pronouncement there is no suggestion of "pie in the sky when you die", and heaven is not our home.

Unlike other faiths the Hebrews did not emphasise escape from the flesh, the attainment of the individual to

Heaven or Nirvana. It apprehended that our planet was the scene of a Divine experiment and the prelude to a further development which could not yet be communicated. This is the burden of the Hebrew Bible and is reflected in primitive Christian teaching. That is why the planetary goal it sets is the resurrection of the body and the conversion of our world to the requirements of the Rule of God. The objective of history is the attainment of heaven upon Earth, as Jesus taught his disciples to pray: "May Thy kingdom come, so that Thy will is done on Earth as it is in Heaven". It is to be a new world of justice, peace and amity, with all nations coming to Zion to be taught about God and His ways. "Nation would no longer lift up sword against nation. Neither would they learn war any more."

In effect resistance to this goal, would be a spur to its attainment, so that unwittingly Evil would be serving the cause of Good. But Evil would also be a hindrance, to be overcome in the course of time by a salutary example, which would display to all mankind what the human race was meant to be and must become, If Man was to fulfil the purpose of his creation. This example would be provided by the Messiah to his Jewish people, and ultimately by this Chosen People to the world.

Thus the message of the Bible is that God knows the End from the Beginning, and is working His purpose out for which our planet was designed. Religions may seek to depict God under many forms and likenesses. The Bible instead seeks to depict Man as God sees him, and to discern His purpose in creating him upon this Earth.

Judaism and Christianity

A Response to the Statement made by Cardinal
Etchegaray [1983] By Dr. Hugh J. Schonfield

The statement made by Cardinal Etchegaray is to be
warmly welcomed as a courageous endeavour to persuade his Church that it has both a religious and historical relationship with the Jewish People, and that
consequently it has an obligation—and indeed a necessity—to promote and cultivate that relationship.

To support his contention the Cardinal draws upon
the Bible, where both in the Old and New Testaments the
permanence of Israel as the People of God is declared.
God is not a human being, who may change his mind
with changes of circumstance. His purposes are unalter-
able. Consequently the Church if it Is representative of
the People of God must be an integral part of Israel. But
how can this be when the greater part of the Church is
composed of non-Jews? The Cardinal cites Romans xi
and Ephesians ii, where it is claimed that all persons
who accept Jesus as Christ (Messiah, the king of Israel)
and give their allegiance to him have become naturalised
Israelites: they have ceased to be Gentiles.

The Cardinal has not made the position sufficiently
clear by wrongly equating Christians with Gentiles. He
should have referred to them as ex-Gentiles. And he fails
to point out that in the Apostolic Age, in the first century
of the Christian Era, the great majority of the followers
of Jesus were Jews whose religion continued to be Judaism. Christianity represented a position within Judaism,
and had not yet become a religion in its own right, a new
independent Faith. The argument of the first century
was not about the relationship between two religions
which had much in common. It was about whether Gen-

tiles who had become Christians could be acknowledged as Israelites.

The issue fills a large part of the Acts of the Apostles and of the Letters of St. Paul. It nearly wrecked the early Church and resulted in a compromise which proved to be unworkable. The witness to it remains in the New Testament; but after two or three centuries the subject ceased to be relevant and Christianity became divorced from Judaism. Neither Church nor Synagogue has been willing to open it again. The matter, therefore, has never been resolved. The question is, Does it have to be? I believe it does, for the sake of Mankind, and not merely of Judaism and Christianity. But I do not think this will happen before the Church has been forced by circumstances to come to the conclusion that it cannot survive, cannot fulfil its destiny, without the Jews. The 'People of God' ideology, if the Bible is to be believed, must prevail one day so that God's will is done on earth as it is in heaven. But it will only happen when there is acknowledgment of One God, One Messiah, and One Israel.

The initiative towards reconciliation has to come from the Church, because it was official Christianity which took the lead in hating and persecuting the Jews, and in misrepresenting them. Even today there is little love for the Jews among leading Churchmen, and the view is sustained that God rejected the Jews and the Christians have taken their place. Cardinal Etchegaray rightly castigates this falsification of the Bible, the Old and the New Testaments. But having affirmed that the Bible knows only one People of God, the People of Israel, the People that was called out of Egypt, given the Torah (the Divine Constitution), and settled in the Promised Land, he fails sufficiently to clarify that Christians, of whatever ethnical origin, are declared to be part of that Israel by faith, and have ceased to be Gentiles.

Really to understand the circumstances we have to go back to the Apostolic Age, and seek to resolve the antique controversy.

In the first century A.D. Judaism was widespread throughout the Roman Empire and beyond. There were synagogues in a great many cities of the pagan world, and worship there was attended by a great many non-Jews, attracted by its purity and the simplicity of the doctrine of One God, invisible, eternal, whom all men could worship. Those who attended also knew that the Jews had been designated as a Priestly People and Holy Nation, governed to this end by special laws which God had given them. There was a choice open to such Gentiles: they could abandon idolatrous paganism while still remaining non-Jews, or they could elect to become Jews by circumcision for males and becoming subject to the Laws of Israel. Both statuses were recognized by the Jews.

The first category were described as "Proselytes of the Gate". They were to be treated by the Jewish Community as the Biblical "Stranger within the Gate", entitled to every care and consideration. Those in the second category were described as "Proselytes of Righteousness". Theirs was a total commitment. They acquired a Jewish identity by baptism and change of name, abandoning all pagan ties and becoming subject to the religious and secular laws of Israel. The "Proselytes of the Gate" had also to agreed to keep certain laws, the so-called Laws of Noah which had applied to the righteous of all nations after the Deluge.

Inevitably, when the Good News (Gospel) that the Messiah of Israel had appeared was proclaimed in the synagogues of the Diaspora by the Jewish apostles this was of great interest to the Gentile Godfearers. They were the most readily persuadable that Jesus was the Christ and wished to join a Christian community. It was specially attractive when St.Paul, as apostle to the Gentiles as he proclaimed himself, ruled that they could become Israelites without undergoing circumcision and the obligations to keep the Mosaic Laws. There had been no provision for such a situation made by the Apostles and Elders in Jerusalem, as an influx of non-Jews into the Church had not been anticipated. They could not entertain that anyone could be entitled to belong to Israel without becoming subject to the laws governing Israel.

This was the real issue. It was not a question of whether Gentiles could follow Jesus without coming under the Mosaic Law. The question was whether Gentiles who did not come under the Law could claim to be Israelites on the basis of being "in Christ". This was what Paul Insisted. For him all who had joined the Church had become naturalised Israelites by faith. He used a kind of rabbinical argument. Since Jesus as Messiah had perfectly kept the whole Law, and at the end had given himself as a sacrifice for sin, all who were in Christ were covered by that sinlessness and sacrifice. What was more, all who were in Christ automatically became Israelites, since Christ was "the seed" (singular) of Abraham (Galatians iii.29).

This kind of argument did not impress the Apostles and Elders who governed the Church in those days, and Paul was required to attend a Council held at Jerusalem. One need not go into the details, but the verdict went against Paul. The Council would not accept his solution. They were willing to rule that Christians from the Gentiles were to be regarded as Proselytes of the Gate if they observed the Laws of Noah (Acts xv.29), but they would not agree to accord them the status of Israelites as Proselytes of Righteousness. The official verdict of the Apostolic Council has never been repealed.

With the destruction by the Romans of all semblance of a Jewish State in A.D.70, and the isolation of the Jewish followers of Jesus in the East from the activities of churches in the West, the issue lost its intensity. Instead there developed another theme, the claim by the Christians that the sufferings of the Jews were a Divine punishment for the crucifixion of Jesus, and that they were now cast off as God's People, and had been replaced by the Church. Though quite unwarranted by the historical facts,as well as by the Bible,this contention has substantially prevailed in the Christian Communions down to the present day. Consequently, a movement in the Churches to acknowledge their error, and the formation of some associations of Christians and Jews, have not made a material difference. Vatican pronouncements have been too equivocal.

It seems to me that, except for an honest expression of deep contrition, the Christians have nothing to say to the Jews until they have put their own house in order. This would require an intensive religious and historical study of Christian Beginnings, which as yet seems unlikely to be forthcoming, at least officially. The Churches must decide whether they still go along with St.Paul. Do they still claim with him that all disciples of Jesus, of whatever origin, are factually members of the People of Israel? Because this was Paul's conviction, continually stated, he could speak of the ancient Israelites as "our fathers" (I. Corinthians x.1-11). If they do make Paul's claim what are the implications of being nationally Israelites, and not in any way a substitute People of God?

Something of tremendous consequence would have happened if the Christians could say to the Jews, "You are our brothers. We share the same ancestry and the same earthly destiny. Collectively we are the People of God." If this situation arose concretely and on a world scale it could not be ignored by the Jewish Community. There would be created a new fluidity with potentially radical adjustments of concepts and interpretations on both sides. The end in view would be the Kingdom of God on Earth, a world of peace and justice such as the prophets of old proclaimed - truly a Messianic Age.

Finally one must say that failure of Jews and Christians at this juncture to carry out their mutual and world obligations does not leave Almighty God without resources. Borrowing from the Bible the spirit of words addressed by Mordecai to Esther (Esther iv.14) one can say, "If you altogether hold your peace at this time, then shall deliverance come to Mankind from another direction."

An Open Letter to Citizens of All Lands

From Sir Anthony Brooke

Fellow citizens,

The world today shows increasing symptoms of perishing for lack of a positive vision, and many of us, it seems to me, are striving to find too much significance and security in rigid identity with dying and changing structures. Confusion is widespread, as is inevitable in a moment of transition from a fast dying epoch to a new dispensation. For all is now to be made new.

My life for the past six years has been one of continuous travel in many lands, meeting and talking with religious, secular and political leaders, with scientists, educationists and specialists of various kinds and, by no means least in importance, with a wide cross-section of a category often called "ordinary citizens"—a term which, although in common usage, tends vastly to underestimate our individual and collective capacity for social effectiveness, as I believe we are soon to discover. It is with this latter category, in individual and group encounters, that I have been spending by far the greater part of my time.

I am shortly to have the privilege of holding, for the period of one year from 28th August, 1966, the office of President of the Commonwealth of World Citizens. But before I take this up I want to share very frankly with you some of my basic convictions and tell you something about the history and functioning of the Commonwealth and why I believe it can be made a particularly effective focus at this time, enabling citizens in all countries greatly to increase their capacities and play a decisive part, not merely in the task of establishing unity and peace in the world, but in ushering in an age for mankind so glorious as to exceed by far our present imaginings.

My reason for wanting to speak of my fundamental beliefs and convictions is because I shall not be simply a figurehead during the year of my Presidency, and although the Commonwealth of World Citizens welcomes citizens of all religious faiths and of none, provided they conform in their thinking and life expression to what the term "world citizen" denotes, it is evident that the dynamic functioning of any individual or group of individuals is crucially affected by the basic beliefs which inspire and motivate them. One might even go so far as to suggest that, when an individual sees himself in relationship with other individuals and his work in the world in a way that transforms him into a fragmented being, cut off from his own deepest motivating convictions, he is scarcely likely to be effective unless he can lay his hands on some external and artificially created powers or props to compensate him for his own inner impoverishment. The history of men, nations and civilizations bears eloquent testimony to the truth of this. Surely it is time we discovered and expressed the spiritual counterpart of nuclear power?

Although many may find it possible, and scientifically acceptable, to do without "God", it is becoming increasingly apparent that something is needed to account for certain rather obscure operations and activities which seem to be taking place in the universe. As an eminent astronomer once remarked: "something unknown is doing we don't know what." Whatever this "Something Unknown" may be, and by whatever name we choose to refer to It, It would seem to merit our very closest attention. For me, it implies at the very least the existence of an intelligent Force which permeates every tiniest atomic particle, seemingly containing the seeds of infinite evolutionary possibilities. I believe that in man this process can become a fully conscious one, and that it is open to man to establish in this generation such an intimate link with this seemingly obscure evolutionary operation as to enable him to become a wholly conscious agent for the next great step which is to bring man nearer to Truth. What I am saying is that I believe in a Plan which at least in part we can know and which we shall presumably desire to know unless we regard our present measure and quality of human wisdom, human knowledge, human power and human love as all sufficing for our needs.

In the world today we have largely turned away from the things which lie beyond our five sense perceptions, and yet it must be acknowledged that if our senses were to embrace a wider range it would be an altogether different universe which we would perceive as actual. In this day of increasing recognition of what has been called extrasensory perception (which may yet be discovered simply as the extension of the range of our natural built-in senses) we are being shaken out of our complacent view of the "material" universe towards a realization that, whether we call it material or spiritual, there is only One Reality which is in some degree apprehensible to us according to the state of our consciousness and of our senses. We may conclude that psychical research is one of the most significant and important branches of investigation ever undertaken by the human mind and it is impossible for our planetary existence to remain unaffected by the dramatic impact of what is coming to light in our time.

While it is unnecessary here to analyse the international situation, or draw detailed attention to the injustices, oppression and widespread poverty and suffering which constitute the condition of by far the greater proportion of humanity today, it is at least intellectually acceptable that this state of affairs could be rapidly changed if only we could find the way to cooperation at all levels on a global scale in place of the existing competition which now so widely prevails. Because of scientific and technological advances, we know that Utopia is, in theory, possible now for the first time in history. We are entering a one-world and space-age society, for which nothing less than a total change in our existing attitudes and structures will prove adequate. Yet I am personally convinced that through the vision and instrumentality of such enterprises as the Commonwealth of World Citizens and above all through impending cosmic happenings calling for our total response, the whole of our planetary existence is quite soon to be changed.

We shall, I believe, and perhaps quite suddenly, awaken to the FACT of One World and of One Indivisible Creation. Our supreme preoccupation from now on should be to prepare our minds and the frameworks of our political and social life for these changes to take place as smoothly as possible.

Origins and Evolution of the Commonwealth of World Citizens

In accordance with scriptural precedent Dr. Hugh J. Schonfield, archaeologist, scholar, lecturer and author of several notable books, in 1938 had a spiritual experience in which he was called, to his own avowed amazement, to "build a nation." It was also revealed to him that the nation in question would, according to the way he later gave expression to the concept, be "a people to serve all peoples, composed of individuals drawn from every land, willing to accept the responsibility of being true world citizens." Their primary loyalty would be given to mankind as a whole, irrespective of race, colour, class or creed, without distinction or discrimination. The new nation would be without armed force, without a territorial homeland, entirely impartial, and in itself a demonstration of world unity. It would be available as an agency to serve by consent in a mediatorial capacity and should be a kind of conscience to the world—a soul, as it were, within the body politic. It would be an adjunct to international organisations, available for service in many ways, having a direct concern for world peace and total human wellbeing. It would exemplify human unity without instituting a world government, and would pioneer a way of evolution from national consciousness to world consciousness, from state loyalty to world loyalty. It would meet a world need which cannot be effectively met by any existing spiritual or secular agency of a restrictive or dogmatic character. It would, above all, pioneer the way of transformation from fragmented living to whole living—from a divided world ruled by expediency and the use of oppressive power to a unified world community, with full scope for diversity, governed by love, truth and the spirit of mutual service.

Following preparatory work by the Servant-Nation Movement, which was brought into being by Dr. Schonfield in 1940, the Commonwealth of World Citizens was founded on 11th November, 1950, and General Assemblies were held in 1950, 1951, 1953 and 1955. At the Constituent Assembly held at Cardiff, Wales, in August 1956, the Commonwealth of World Citizens was formally brought to birth as a nation, and the Moncivitan Republic ("Mondcivitano" being Esperanto for "World Citizen") duly came into existence. In 1952 there were Citizens in 14 countries: in 1954 in 25 countries. By 1962 there were Citizens in 60 countries.

Administrative Structure

In accordance with the Articles of the Constitution a Supreme Council, consisting of five elected Citizens is reconstituted every five years, and the Presidency of the Council is held by each member in turn for the period of one year. The Mondcivitan Republic has relations with existing governments and with the United Nations. An agency of the Republic, the World Service Trust, founded in 1955, exists for the purpose of giving aid to people and countries in circumstances of poverty, famine, disease, epidemics and natural disasters. It sometimes initiates projects and at other times works in collaboration with United Nations agencies, the International Red Cross and appropriate humanitarian organisations.

The Mondcivitan Republic provides means of association with fellow Citizens and requires participation in the self-government of the Republic locally and universally by vote, and devotion of time to its affairs according to opportunity. It also requires payment of an annual contribution. The present rate of recommended contribution is 1% of personal net income, but Citizens are expected to determine for themselves what they feel should be their just individual contribution.

Consisting as it does of a republic of world citizens, the Mondcivitan Republic has parliamentary representation but no political parties or a party line. It aims to be an integrated and harmonious planetary society capable of inspiring international cooperation and goodwill. The terms "republic", "nation", "parliament", "government", "ministers" and "citizens" are all constitutionally applicable to the functioning of the Mondcivitan Republic. The only term in international usage which is not applicable is "state", because this would imply functioning in a separate country of their own, which, for World Citizens of the Commonwealth, is neither possible nor permissible. The world is at present divided into twenty electoral zones, according to the distribution of Citizens, with two deputies returnable for each zone. The last election was held in 1963.

It is to be hoped that nation-states will come increasingly to appreciate the rightness and advantage of releasing their citizens from enforced compliance with any policies harmful to any section of humanity, in order that this initial minority of World Citizens, broadly distributed over the face of the globe, may be encouraged effectively to play their part as true peacemakers in helping to bring about a condition on earth to which all peoples and nations openly and avowedly aspire. Meanwhile, World Citizens of the Commonwealth are required to respect and comply with the laws of the countries in which they live, it being a matter for individual conscience when a Citizen is confronted with a law which in his understanding is injurious to the world community.

The terms and conditions of citizenship are what any nation-state chooses to make them and it is fully within the competence of every state to allow a citizen to hold World Citizenship within the Commonwealth.

The Immediate Task Ahead

Our needs, simply stated, are first and foremost to secure widespread recognition of the fact that the Commonwealth of World Citizens exists, and what it signifies. If you are sympathetic, you can help greatly by bringing this letter to the attention of the editors of local newspapers and of those operating radio and television services. You might consider bringing it to the attention of the public spirited individuals of your acquaintance, especially those engaged in civic and educational activity. Together with this, there is an urgent need to locate those citizens in all countries who have become awakened to the realization that true thinking and sane thinking require, by an act of will, our living and acting together as world citizens. This process has already begun, and as world citizens link up with one another in their immediate vicinity they can, individually and in small units become a significant and dynamic focal point of influence. Experience shows that the ideal unit comprises between five and ten persons, but quite small units can also be extremely effective. Indeed, a single, dedicated world citizen, if there are none others initially at hand with whom to link, can alone make a powerful impact.

Although there should be no delay in world citizens operating on their own initiative and in accordance with their own inspired ideas for furthering the cause of world citizenship, it is open to all to apply for admission to the Mondcivitan Republic. This in effect means that in due course they will receive a simple form inviting them outwardly to acknowledge their inner resolution, and the way will thereby be opened for more effective participation through the activities and unifying agencies of the Commonwealth of World Citizens. Let this, however, be clearly understood. The Commonwealth is the sum of its Citizens, both as regards size and quality. Each Citizen is expected to be an embryonic "headquarters" in himself, and this concept extends also to every unit that comes into being. It is a two way flow—the main emphasis at this stage being communication and coordination.

The power and effectiveness of the Commonwealth of World Citizens lie primarily in the devotion of those Citizens whose predominant concern is to manifest their own highest vision of life and relationship, grounded and made effective through their direct link with the transforming energies now coming upon the earth to bring it to new light and into a new dispensation. I personally feel that this "direct link" can best be established in the Silence, shared if possible with one or two others, when the five senses become stilled and the higher sense perceptions possessed by every one of us are accordingly given an opportunity to enrich and amplify our capacities for wise and effective individual and collective action.

A noted scholar, speaking of our human dilemma, once made the following striking observation:

"It may be that, just when confusion is at its height and about to break out into conflict, the clamour will be hushed by the sudden trumpet-call to a new enterprise for humanity—I mean, by the unexpected emergence of some commanding aim, of an overarching purpose that would capture the imaginations of multitudes, drown their quarrels, override their disputes, make them ashamed of their former petty-mindedness, and carry them forward on a tidal wave of magnanimous resolve to an end worth attaining by man."

Mighty changes are on the way and the call has gone forth to the ends of the earth. A new world is in the making. Man's opportunity has never been greater. One question alone remains.

Are we or are we not, individually and collectively, to unite consciously with that Great Universal Force which, like the power at the core of the atom, has lain dormant deep in everyone of us from the beginning of time, and so participate in the glorious transformation of our planet and of all life on earth?

ANTHONY BROOKE.

Biographical Note

Anthony Brooke is a descendant of Sir James Brooke, who in 1841 became known as the first "White Rajah" of Sarawak. Three generations of Mr. Brooke's family ruled the country as an independent sovereign state for just over a hundred years, until it became a British colony in 1946 and subsequently, in 1963, entered the Federation of Malaysia. Anthony Brooke, as Rajah Muda of Sarawak, ruled for a period in 1939, and after World War II he campaigned constitutionally for five years with Sarawak nationalists against the transformation of the territory into a British colony.

In recent years Anthony Brooke has been linking with different groups throughout the world having a special concern for unity and peace and education for world citizenship. He is a Member of the Supreme Council of the Commonwealth of World Citizens and a Vice-President of World Union: a life member of the Royal Institute of International Affairs (Chatham House), International Fellowship of Reconciliation, Churches' Fellowship for Psychical and Spiritual Study, Spiritual Frontiers Fellowship, Society for Psychical Research: a member of Fellowship of Friends of Truth and of the

Wider Quaker Fellowship. An Esperantist. He is author of the pamphlets "The Time is Now" (1965) and "Are These The Signs?" (1966).

H. G. Wells—Prophet and Seer

The chief debt which I owe to the writings of H. G. Wells is that he fired my imagination and compelled me to concern myself in practical terms with the future of humanity.

Many of my own, the older, generation of today would say that his work had a like effect on them.

By the end of the nineteenth century, when, as a result of illness, Wells at about thirty years of age became committed to a literary career, the past of our planet had amazingly come alive through the remarkable investigations of scientists and archaeologists. The present was prosperous, eager and questing, full of invention, development and reform. Not many minds ranged far ahead, probing, evaluating, discerning prospects that were not inevitably those of peace and perfection.

The Bible tells us that he who is now called a prophet was in an older time called a seer. Wells was a seer. His eyes, as I remember them when I came to know him personally, were those of a visionary. He did not so much predict as employ an alert not easily imposed upon brain to detect ruthlessly tile consequences of the behaviour of the human animal. And this he did in no spirit of misanthropy, but with a passionate care for mankind. His anticipations, and this could not be otherwise, were often wrong in detail, and his hopes, reflecting a faith that was religious though partaking of no religion, sometimes gave men too great a benefit of his rational doubt; but in his perception of trends and potentialities his vision was frequently uncannily correct.

One of the reasons for the paradox that so many of his books are unread today, while his name remains one to conjure with, is perhaps that the limes in which we now live are so extraordinarily Wellsian. We have come with justification to apply his name adjectivally to circumstances akin to those his fertile imagination described.

We might well question, in a nice juggling with concepts of time and space such as he loved, whether the real world is not pursuing its course quite differently on another plane of existence, while the one we are experiencing is a fiction conceived by Herbert George Wells.

Wells was responsible for some of the earliest essays in what is commonly called science-fiction, and his greatest output of books and stories in this field was in the period 1895-1901. There were *The Time Machine* (recently filmed), *The Wonderful Visit*, *The Stolen Bacillus and Other Incidents* (all in 1895). *The Island of Dr. Moreau and* The Wheels of Chance followed in 1896. The *Invisible Man*, *The Planner Story and Others* and *Thirty Strange Stories* came in 1897. The *War of the Worlds* appeared in 1898; When *the Sleeper Wakes* in 1899, and The *First Men in the Moon* in 1901. Some of these are still popular.

But unlike much that passes for science-fiction nowadays, these products of Wells's creative genius were not meant simply to astound or terrify: they had a didactic and sociological significance. Wells was a teacher of men about mankind. The strangest of his tales has verisimilitude. His characters are normally those of orderly lower middle and professional classes, more emotionally affected by untoward events and more capable of a reasoning reaction to surprising experiences. What takes place, however fantastic, is usually in localities unremarkable in their propriety and sobriety. It is this impingement of the extravagant upon the commonplace which evokes a thoughtful response in the reader. To illustrate, I instance three of the books mentioned.

The Time Machine is launched from Richmond, Surrey, into the year 802,701 A.D. At the same spot in this remote future, the Time Traveller finds above-ground an elegant child-like race, the Eloi, while below-ground operating machines in the depths are the loathsome lemur-like race of Morlocks. The Traveller muses on what might have happened to account for this phenomenon.

The upper-world people might once have been the favoured aristocracy, and the Morlocks their mechanical servants; but that had long since passed away. The two species that had resulted from the evolution of man were sliding down towards, or had already arrived at, an altogether new relationship... The Nemesis of the delicate ones was creeping on apace. Ages ago, thousands of generations ago, man, had thrust his brother man out of the ease and the sunshine. And now that brother was coming back—changed!

Another aspect of the thesis is presented in *The Island of Dr. Moreau*. Edward Prendick is shipwrecked on a strange island, where the half-mad surgeon Moreau is torturing animals into the semblance of human beings, teaching them to speak and be obedient to the Law. At first Prendick makes the natural mistake that it is humans whom the doctor is bestialising; but he soon learns that the object of the experiments is to burn out the animal and create from beasts rational beings. But so far they always revert to their former nature. The horror of the story makes almost a light comedy of Orwell's much later Animal Farm. Finally the doctor is killed and Prendick escapes. But he returns to civilisation a doomed man.

My trouble took the strangest form. I could not persuade myself that the men and women I met were not also another, still passably human, Beast People, animals half-wrought into the outward image of human souls, and that they would presently begin to revert, to show first this bestial mark and then that... I would go out into the streets to fight with my delusion and prowling women would mew after me, furtive craving men glance jealously at me... Then I would turn aside into some-chapel and even there, such was my disturbance, it seemed that the preacher gibbered Big Thinks even as the Ape Man had done.

Still another approach is offered in The War of the Worlds, in which Martian invaders equipped with vastly superior death-dealing weapons, land initially in Surrey. Nothing can stop them. The world of men is fated to become cattle for the Martial overlords. But the hero encounters an artilleryman on Putney Hill, who has got everything worked out.
We have to invent a sort of life where man can live and breed, and be sufficiently secure to bring the children up... You see, how I mean to live is under-ground... The main drains are big enough and airy enough for anyone. But saving the race is nothing in itself. As I say, that's only being rats. It's saving our knowledge and adding to it is the thing... After all. it may not be so much we have to learn before — just imagine this:
Four or five of their Fighting Machines suddenly starting off Heat Rays right and left, and not a Mar-tian in 'em. Not a Martian in 'em, but men—men who have learnt the way how... and, behold! Man has come back to his own.

The man who could write such things before the development of ideological conflict, before the invention of nuclear weapons and the devising of underground radiation proof shelters, the man who dared to look steadily down the long corridors of time, was no ordinary man or writer.

H. G. Wells was born at Bromley, Kent, in 1866. He died just short of his eightieth birthday on August 13th, 1946. His father ran a hardware shop in the High Street, and though H.G. had a fair schooling and was an enthusiast for self-education he served two years as an apprentice to a draper in Southsea, experiences of trade which find echoes in Kipps (1905) and *The History of Mr. Polly* (1910). But he broke away, and was able to pursue scientific studies—which he put to good service in his books —at what is now the Imperial College of Science, Kensington. For a few years thereafter he was a schoolmaster and tutor until ill-health brought him to full-time authorship and fame.

The novels which mirror his own life and times have a continuing and endearing place in the long list of his published works.

Memorable, besides the two just mentioned, were *Love and Mr. Lewisham* (1900), *Tono Bungay and Anne Veronica* (in 1909). His versatility, as his bibliography testifies, was quite amazing.

But principally Wells was the seer and educator, beginning with *Mankind in the Making* (1903), continuing with the memorable *Outline of History*, which I devoured excitedly in my youth when it began to appear in 1919 in fortnightly parts, and culminating (in collaboration) with *The Work, Wealth and Happiness of Mankind* (1932) and the *Science of Life* series initiated in 1935. One of his hopes, as yet unrealised, was for the institution of a *World Encyclopaedia*. Not to be forgotten is his dramatic fictional forecast The *Shape of Things to Come* (1933), since filmed and broadcast.

The challenges of the world situation following the first world war stimulated Wells, and set him intensively to planning as well as predicting. The Gospel of Wells was formulated cogently in *The Open Conspiracy* (1928) and its successors.

Now, while one day he would be wearing the mantle of the prophet, the next, metaphorically, he would be striding out, staff in hand, as the evangelist of his own message, and this went on throughout the second world war in which he called for a fresh declaration of *The Rights of Man*. He was as forceful and as uncompromising as any revivalist, and occasionally, discarding the written word, his thin piping voice would be heard on public platforms.

Wells had always been himself in everything he recorded, and in his later years he may be forgiven for seeming something of a know-all and inclined to rudeness, though privately the kindest of men. Arrant stupidity infuriated him, and he found unresponsiveness hard to bear. He had been right so often; but his strong dislikes could lead him astray.

He believed in World Government and World Citizenship, but most unconventionally. He came to fashion a Wellsiocentric universe, a kind of projection of himself into the world around him. He visualised a planet peopled with Wellsians, alert hard far-ranging minds like his own, carrying out his programme of World Revolution.

Phoenix, published in 1942, concluded dogmatically: "In this book we have assembled the whole complete case for a rational World Reconstruction. Every part of it interlocks and depends on every other part. Take it or leave it. *There is no other way*" (Wells's italics). It oppressed him at the close of his life, and he expressed it in *Mind at the End of its Tether* (1946), that it looked as if the post-war world would opt to "leave it". But who could tell? Man, pursuing his arduous ascent, might yet find the way pioneered by H. G. Wells of service to him, and so come in due time to the summit of fulfilment.

By purely literary standards Wells was not a great writer, though some of his passages and stories have the quality of greatness. But he did write greatly and about great issues, purveying a yeast that will cause much ferment yet. We are far from done with him.

Reprinted from John o' London's, 28th September, 1961

The Gandhi Centenary

This Spring [1969] the centenary of the birth of Mahatma Gandhi will be universally celebrated. In the little Mediterranean island of Malta where I have been recently they have marked the occasion by the issue of a special portrait postage stamp. But to honour great men is not the same thing as heeding what they have to teach. Gandhi helped effectively to give India its independence; but his method of operation had universal significance. He will be chiefly remembered for promoting the technique of non-violence and for his insistence that behind political action there must be Ahimsa (positive outgoing love).

Many who were followers of Gandhi were fully prepared to hero-worship him as a patriot and a saint, but not to put his teaching into effect. Today many resistance groups identify themselves with non-violence in their demonstrations, but what has become of Ahimsa! One does not hear much of it in the protesting voices which are raised.

Political action is valid, and indeed essential, but in the spirit of Gandhi its aim must be to win over opponents through love. The Mondcivitan Republic is committed completely to what Gandhi represented in refusing to acknowledge anyone as an enemy. With us world citizenship is united with love towards all mankind, including those whose methods and behaviour are selfish, cruel and unjust. Often it is not easy to believe that they can be changed. But we have to recognise that there is in them a divine spark which is capable of making a response. If it were not so the cause of humanity would be hopeless, and all our endeavours to transform the world would be vain.

There is another lesson to be learnt from Gandhi's story. Individuals can set an example, but there is little they can do practically without the full cooperation of those who are likeminded. The saviour figure is too often used as an excuse for inactivity, and there is too much dependence on leadership. When Gandhi died so tragically there were too few who could take his place, and little by little there was a reversion to the old and undesirable forms of relationships. The only way to avoid such a contingency in any movement is by having a common cause with the widest possible distribution of responsibility. Whenever an office is laid down there must always be someone ready to take it over. Where there are real convictions this should present no difficulty, and this is what is involved when we speak of ourselves as a Republic. We are not anyone's followers or supporters, and the cause we serve is that of us all equally.

From The World Citizen Spring 1969

The Historical Jesus in The Passover Plot Approach

Through the instrumentality of the Christian Church a certain Jesus who lived nearly two thousand years ago, and who was crucified by the Romans at Jerusalem, became the central figure of a new religious cult, as the Christian creed superseded the pagan religions of the West the potency of the Jesus Faith increased: it established him for multitudes as God incarnate in a human being to save mankind by suffering for their sins.

The accounts of him, handed down in the Gospels, were credited implicitly as Divinely inspired. This is still the position of conservative Christians.

But in modern times freedom of thought and inquiry has called in question the interpretations of Christian orthodoxy and the veracity of the Gospel records. Scientific investigation and research has been directed to seeking to discover what can be learnt of the historical Jesus, the man behind the myth. The effect has certainly not been to destroy the importance, even the uniqueness, of Jesus for the world of today. Christianity has assured that his image as a consequential figure remains indelible. His name and prestige is enlisted accordingly in the service of many causes and viewpoints, spiritual, social and political. He is still, sometimes in strange and exotic guises, the leader and exemplar for the inspiration of many.

What has been weakened is the theological interpretation of the person and purpose of Jesus, especially since it has been demonstrated that the Gospels are largely secondary sources of information which betray both the growth of legend and a radical change in Christian thought and concerns.

This has opened the door to various views of Jesus, often with little or no justification historically. Largely they take Jesus out of the context of his native environment and are alien to his character as a devout Jew.

Indeed, it may be said that it has been the Jewishness of Jesus which has been the principle obstacle to comprehending him. Since 70 A.D., when Judea was overwhelmed by the Roman legions, Christianity has existed predominantly in a Gentile environment which has been strongly antisemitic. Consequently very few Christian scholars have been able to bring themselves to think of Jesus primarily and objectively as a Jew, thus destroying the possibility of comprehending him accurately. For Christians, Jesus was depicted as superhuman with a mission to mankind, one who had suffered for the sins of the whole world. His teaching superseded Judaism, and his own people opposed and rejected him, and finally procured his death. That Jesus had been born a Jew was an unfortunate prophetic necessity.

Yet the oldest factual evidence we have witnesses to the total Jewishness of Jesus and his exclusive commitment to his own nation. This evidence is furnished by the title Christ attached to his name in the very earliest sources. Christ is from the Greek translation of the Hebrew title Messiah (the anointed one), denoting, as even the Gospels admit, the expected Jewish king of the Jews of the house of David who would arise at the appointed time. It was for the crime against Caesar of claiming the Jewish crown that Jesus was crucified.

There were many Jews called Jesus (i.e. Joshua) in those days; but only one of them was known as Christ. The Jewish historian Josephus witnesses to this. The Messiah (Christ) was to be a pious Jew of David's line, who would serve God faithfully and uphold His Law. He would be invested with the Divine Spirit, which would confer upon him wisdom and understanding as a model prince. His initial task would be to lead his people back to God, so that restored to their land they would become an inspiration to all nations, who then would abandon their idolatry and turn to Jerusalem for instruction in God's ways. The

Gentiles would not readily accept God's rule initially, and Judgments would fall on their hostile hosts as in ancient times they had fallen upon the Egyptians. This is what the Prophets of Israel had foreseen, and the interpreters of their words had elaborated before Jesus was born.

In coming to the conviction that God had destined him to be the Messiah the young Jesus would have seen his function solely as reflecting these anticipations. We are not entitled to go outside these terms of reference in seeking to comprehend him and the manner in which he sought to fulfil his task. If we do we are opposing the truth and our view of Jesus will be unrealistic and unhistorical.

Naturally, this is anathema to the theologians, and to all who cannot bear to think of Jesus as a Jewish Messiah. They try to get round the unwelcome idea in three ways. What Jesus was for the Jews is of no interest to the rest of mankind, who not having Jewish scruples are able to worship him as God incarnate, a far superior status. Alternatively, Jesus was alien to Jewish teaching, and revealed himself as a very different kind of Messiah to that which the Jews were expecting. (The theologians do not observe that they are accusing Jesus of fraud, since if he presented himself in another guise he was deliberately deceiving his people and their rejection of him would be fully justified). A third position is one of evasion. Jesus made no claim to be the Messiah: it was his Jewish disciples who made this claim on his behalf; and since the Jewish Christians ceased to be of any consequence after the destruction of Jerusalem by the Romans what they believed does not affect the Church's teaching, (in none of the Creeds are Christians asked to affirm that Jesus is the Messiah).

What may be thought by Christians to be doctrinally relevant has no title to be imposed on our understanding of the Jesus of history. Indeed, it is a positive impediment to understanding since it inhibits objective and unbiassed inquiry.

Many are on the horns of a dilemma, because the Gospels speak with two voices which are often contradictory.

They speak at one time of a near and at another of a more remote return of Jesus and the coming of the Kingdom of God on earth. It is declared that Jesus violated the Law and also taught rigid adherence to it. It is said that Jesus came only to his own nation and at the same time cast them aside. Jesus insists that his apostles should go to none but Jews, but after his resurrection is made to tell them to preach in all the world to everyone.

As a result of the literary study of the Gospels these contradictions are readily explained. They represent earlier and later positions. None of the four Gospels was written in Palestine, and all of them were composed after the war between the Jews and the Romans at various dates between 75 A.D. and the end of the first century or beginning of the second. In order of appearance they bear the names of Mark, Matthew, Luke, John, and were published in different parts of the Roman Empire. The names reflect distinctive elements in the contents, which can be dated back before the Jewish War. Some traditions about this have been preserved.

Mark (i.e. John Mark of Jerusalem) is said to have been the apostle Peter's interpreter during his missionary travels, and to have made notes of what Peter had reported of things said and done by Jesus. Mark later published these collected notes, but was not concerned to represent the events in strict chronological order. Our Mark used this lost document as a primary source, which gave the resultant Gospel its name.

Matthew, one of the Twelve, is credited with compiling two small works in Hebrew, one a collection of Old Testament passages regarded as predictions of the circumstances relating to Jesus as Messiah, and the other a collection of the teachings of Jesus. These documents are also lost; but

Matthew's Gospel used them as well as Mark as source material.

Luke was a medical man who accompanied the apostle Paul on many of his journeys. He appears to have been a

Gentile who either partially or wholly had embraced Judaism. The 'we' passages in the Acts of the Apostles may well be part of a diary kept by him, and Luke's Gospel is said by tradition to reflect Paul's preaching. The author of the Gospel and the Acts claims to have carried out a thorough research of Christian beginnings, and Dr. Luke's material may well have been one of his sources, as well as Mark, Matthew's teaching document, and other available traditions.

The unnamed Beloved Disciple of John's Gospel was not one of the Twelve (the Church confuses him with one of the sons of Zebedee), but a man of some note in Jerusalem, probably of priestly family, who before he met Jesus had been a follower of John the Baptist. In extreme old age at Ephesus he was persuaded to dictate his recollections of Jesus. These were utilised by the Greek author of John's Gospel, who may also have been called John, who composed discourses attributed to Jesus and much explanatory teaching of an alien unjewish character.

The underlying sources were very important for the Gospel writers, since this gave them a claim to authority among Christians of their time and helped to make their own ideas and convictions acceptable to their contemporaries. Scholarship can substantially distinguish early from late elements by their Hebraic structure and Jewishness of sentiment and scene, and it is upon this early material that we must rely to the exclusion of the rest for access to the Jesus of history. In doing so we are not employing what suits us, but what is evidently more closely related to the actual circumstances.

There is of course much more to the study of Christian origins than is indicated here, but this illustrates the guide lines.

We have resolutely to eliminate from our concept of Jesus the alterations and additions which transformed his image and status, and bring to bear on the earlier material such knowledge of the conditions and circumstances at the time of Jesus (the first third of the first century A.D.) as may be gleaned from non-Biblical Jewish and non-Jewish sources. This is particularly important for comprehending Jesus' understanding of the Messianic as applying to himself and his function, and also for apprehending contemporary reactions politica1, religious and social.

A very clear and consistent picture of Jesus emerges from such investigation, and his actions from beginning to end make complete sense, he is a man of high intelligence, imagination and determination, with a personality very easy to grasp when we cease to think of him as superhuman. He is a devout and spiritual Jew, but very much a Jew, one with a prophetic vision obsessed with the implications of what he is sure is his calling to be the Messianic leader and deliverer of his people. He is a man with intense feelings of love and compassion; but his devotion to the Mosaic Law and his Messianic task makes nonsense of suggestions that he had any irregular sexual experiences. He is also a man with strong emotions of joy and sorrow, anger and contempt. At the same time his faith is passionate and positive.

He is extremely observant of what is going on about him, and acquainted with contemporary conditions and events. He is a very good judge of character and knows how to deal with people. Convinced that he is the Messiah, though careful not to divulge his identity prematurely, he speaks with an authority which is disturbing and even resented by those of recognised position and power. Jesus is quick-witted with a very active and resourceful brain, a born strategist able to counter the moves of his opponents and compel them to do what he wants. He perceives his destiny clearly and dramatically in accordance with the interpretation of the Scriptures prophetically, especially the experiences of his ancestor David as related in the books of Samuel and the Psalms, and plans to bring to pass what must be fulfilled, with a mind alert to every detail.

Jesus emerges from such intense study and scrutiny as a most exceptional and remarkable individual, in many respects unique because the function he accepted as his was unique. If he was deceiving anyone it could only be himself, and who is to say whether what he believed about himself was true or false? Some may say he was mad, others that he was a genius. But certainly he was a man, and essentially—perhaps to Gentiles uncomprehendingly—a Jew, and no God-man. Such a man was only possible in his own time and land.

This is the true Jesus, who—when he is perceived - can have his story told, as in THE PASSOVER PLOT, with great fidelity, in keeping with the precious recollections of him which the Gospel writers almost against their will have preserved. This was the one who claimed to be the Messiah of Israel, the awaited king of the Jews, and who is to be apprehended and judged in that light alone.

Why should the world trouble itself about such a Jew? Apart from the obvious reasons, it may be because he alone holds the secret of the ultimate peace and harmony of mankind!

Symposium at the Université Holistique

June 25-26, Paris, France 1982

Hugh J. Schonfield's First Contribution

Mr. President, Colleagues and Friends, I have to speak in English to make myself clearly understood, and I want to introduce at the end of the day a note of optimism to bring things into perspective. I am a young man (only 82 years of age) and it is within my lifetime that mankind has penetrated into every part of this planet, which he had never done before. It was when I was a boy that the North Pole and the South Pole were visited for the first time, and it is only recently that we have seen our world from the outside, viewed from Space. So you will appreciate that we now have to look at things a little differently, in a whole context.

In the Bible, it says that one day is with the Lord as a thousand years. According to that reckoning, the human race is about six years old. It is from this viewpoint that we have to see things, so that we do not frighten ourselves. We have a long long way to go yet, and we are only just beginning to learn how to move forward.

For ages we have had the wonderful capacity to see how our world, how things, appear when we view them in three dimensions. But a three-dimensional world cannot tell us for what purpose something exists. I can look at a machine in three dimensions, but unless I am informed or I am familiar with it I may not be aware of its purpose. To illustrate in the simplest terms. Someone might come to our world from outer space and see a chair. We know that you sit on it; but the visitor may think that you stand on it. As yet we are trying to solve our problems with a three- dimensional vision. We have now to introduce a fourth dimension, to ask for what purpose something is there? What purpose does it serve? What is its object? It is like this with the human race. How can we deal correctly with our problems and our difficulties unless we know why we are here?

So now we have to introduce into our thinking, and to apply, a fourth dimension with reference to our human relationships. Some people have thought of Time as this dimension. But if everything was in the dimension of Time we could only see it for an instant. So Time cannot be our fourth dimension. Because God is timeless He is invisible. So our fourth dimension, I would suggest, has to be the purpose for which a thing is made, for which it is created, for which it exists, what function it performs. We cannot perceive that simply by vision: we need an analytical dimension. In that direction we turn to the Bible. Please understand that this is not a book of religion: it is the Book of the Story of Man, from the primeval Garden to the Ultimate City, and this city for all mankind is described as a cube: it is fourth-dimensional, and it is this additional dimension that we are now having to begin to think of almost for the first time.

So now we are seeking to Introduce a fourth dimension into our international affairs and into our relationships in industry. We are saying that we have to have somebody, an individual, organization or group, not a party to disputes, who can bring people together who are opposing one another by seeing the circumstances as a whole, what the trouble is really about. The United Nations has part of that responsibility to-day, to reconcile the opposing aims and attitudes of its individual members by creating something which is part of them all, but also stands apart from them all. So our task today, as we begin to see our world as a whole, is also to begin to see humanity as a whole.

What is the use of saying, "Let us have this kind of organization, or that kind of organization," when we do not know where we are going? We have to start right at the beginning. What is humanity for? Why is man on this planet? What purpose does he serve? What is his function? Only when we have some answer to such questions can we understand how we should proceed.

This is why there are organizations like Holism. It is a holistic attitude to seek to see things in their entirety, to see them whole. That means trying to see things with God's eyes, inside and outside. It has now become essential for some part of humanity to begin to cultivate a Wholeness consciousness.

When I was a boy there was a very great writer, H. G. Wells. I expect some of you have read some of his books. One of them came out first in fortnightly parts: it was called The Outline of History. Before that our history books were looking at the world from the viewpoint of the various nations to which we belonged. He said that we must now look at the whole story of mankind embracing all nations. Then perhaps we can begin to see where all mankind is going. And this is the perspective that we have to cultivate today.

We need volunteers, prepared to undergo the difficult and very exacting task of learning to look at things whole, to see our world as a whole.

And we have to do this not with the idea of Mastery, which is largely the fashion with world outlooks; but rather as Servants of all mankind. If our planet is to become one to our vision, it has also to become one to our hearts and lives.

The destiny of mankind rests on the shoulders of such people. Some of us have the responsibility of being an advance guard of the rest of humanity. And here I would remind you of words that Jesus used, when he said, "You don't take a lamp and put it under a cover. You set it on a lampstand, that it may give light to all who are in the house." He also said that "a city which stands on a hilltop cannot be hidden." It functions the other way also. With the light we can see the whole room, and from the hilltop we can view the whole landscape.

So now It is demanded of us to acquire the perspective that sees things whole, as the sum of all the parts, and which sees ourselves as the servants of that whole, so that we may go forward and become increasingly accustomed to the concept of unity. We have to learn how to detach ourselves from many problems which trouble us. And when we have that detachment then to direct ourselves to solving them, and not before. This is the task and the responsibility of the WHOLENESS viewpoint.

Replies to Questions

The question of power has of course to be faced. We are living in an age in which remarkable discoveries of new sources of power have been made.

This has rather gone to our heads. And, consequently, it is not easy for us at this stage to view things intelligently. I tried to indicate to you how young we are, and we need much more training yet before we really know how to deal with our problems. We can see, or ought to see, that there are two sides we have always to be concerned with, one is involvement, and the other is detachment. We have to unite the two, so that we are in total sympathy with the problems we are dealing with, and sufficiently detached from them to see the possibilities of a solution.

I would stress that we are only at the beginning of this experience of seeing things whole. That is why we must not ask or expect too much from the international agencies we have created. What I am satisfied about is that our troubles will not destroy us.

Of course we cannot go on indefinitely in the way we have been doing. We must come to a stop. But you cannot stop before you clearly discern what you have to do. First you have to be clear where you are going, what you are seeking to create. If I start on a journey with no purpose in view, how will I know what things I am going to need? We tend to think that anyone without special competence can leap at a successful solution to our problems.

Hugh J. Schonfield's Second Contribution

Thank you, Madame President.

You have referred to me as a Prophet of the New Age. Well, you can see that I can see into the future because I was very careful to bring my raincoat with me.

What I wanted to begin to do yesterday was to introduce into our Conference an atmosphere of optimism, and some here have helped me in this. I suggested that in the time sequence the human race has now reached about six years of age. It is a very important age. It is the age when not only as an individual does one begin to learn from a teacher, but also to live and learn in a society, in a school, in conjunction with others. And this is equally essential, this learning how to live together, as the learning about things that relate to the human story. We are beginning today the movement into Space, but we also have to learn how to move in Time, and therefore increasingly to be able to see things in their wholeness.

We have not yet reached the point where we can send people ahead of us into the future to seek the help of our descendants to take us forward safely. But I do want to stress that there is a Higher Power, Who, long before the creation of Han, knew the end from the beginning. And it was a good end. So that we have not to be afraid of the circumstances we encounter in this world.

Of course we have to be concerned, we have to be involved, because it is our story that is being told, our contribution. But we have not to fear, we have not to be anxious, that we will end up with destruction. What we will finish with is a Greater Life. This is something that our age has particularly to be concerned with in view of the nuclear threat that hangs over us, that we are not at the end of our history. But we are at a turning point in our history.

We are moving now out of the period which has been concerned with the international to go forward towards the universal in the affairs of our planet. The new period began seriously in the seventeenth century as a consequence of the Thirty Years War. As a result of that terrible experience a man called Hugo Grotius (Hugh de Groot) wrote a great work entitled The Law of War and Peace (De Jure Belli ac Pacis) in which he saw that there had to be an Instrument of arbitration in the relations between states to restore harmony between opposing sides in circumstances of conflict. This need is something we are increasingly beginning to appreciate.

Here, in Paris, I would like to take you back to the end of the eighteenth century, the time of the French Revolution. This was the beginning of Man thinking of himself as a human being in his own right, as distinct from an individual who was a member of a particular class, or of a particular state. Mankind was beginning to see that persons could reach out to one another for purposes and interests they had in common across frontiers and classes in many connections, whether in science, or the arts, or in social and political activities, whatever it might be. There was, for example, in the conception of Communism the call for the workers of the world to unite.

Thus for the first time in a positive way the idea of the Brotherhood of Man was beginning to be appreciated. And since that time we have been seeking to move progressively forward towards a greater international understanding and the discovery of common objectives for the human race.

And we began to discover that we had common responsibilities in relation to our planet. For the first time we began to look at our world as a whole, and not as a collection of separate parts. And this universal outlook is the thing that we have been trying seriously, all of us here, to acquire.

We are now living much more positively in a world environment, and we have been trying to move in this direction through our institutions. It was to this end that there was created the League of Nations, and later the United Nations. This was a remarkable advance, in some ways more remarkable than perhaps some of us have appreciated.

We were to have in the Secretariat and permanent officials of the United Nations people who were detached from representing their own countries in order to represent all the member countries. There was created a kind of international civil service, something that never existed before. And there were also created Specialised Agencies concerned with the various problems and needs arising from sharing the same planet.

These have illustrated the way in which we have begun to move forward, forward now from an international towards a universal approach, to a world approach, to common ends and circumstances.

But the process has to involve a further stage of development. Our conference this week-end is an illustration of it. We have come together from our various positions, but all of us with a common concern for the whole of mankind and how we can build for the future.

To that end there has been need for a certain detachment as well as a certain involvement. God sees things whole; but it is difficult for man to see things whole in terms of our planet. So not only have we to take those stages forward represented by bodies like the United Nations, we have to have this further new concept of being citizens of the world, representatives of the whole human race.

And this human race has, as it were, to send into the future a kind of advance guard or scouting party in order to be able to come back and tell us which is the best way to go forward. This body of pioneers has to be a kind of offering which every nation makes in the interests of the whole, the donation of some of its people to mankind at large. And in the next stage of our human development this enterprise will be the primary necessity and activity.

So now, first of all, we have to have that minority which begins to move into the area of wholeness. Even now we can see how vital this is, because we have disputes, not only international disputes, but also industrial disputes, involving also class and race. We are seeing the need to have groups or individuals who are not involved in the issues, but comprehend them, to seek without prejudice to bring the opposing parties together and resolve their differences. Such mediators have to see situations in a wider context than the partisan positions people take, and therefore to propose ways of reconciliation.

This function is an essential part now of the development of a world citizenship. As I have said, we have to move forward from internationalism to universalism. And this calls for some of us to begin to see things whole in order to help mankind to move forward into that wholeness, which it cannot achieve at one jump as imagined by the advocates of world government and world federation.

A very grave responsibility is laid on people who claim to be world- minded. The emphasis has not to be on a personal self-development but on an identification with our fellows, on history as a whole, as the story of mankind. Without this we cannot discern its purpose and objectives, we cannot tell where we are going. And therefore we cannot lead the way forward into the future and guide the people of our time in the right direction.

In order to climb Mount Everest there had to be people who had submitted to a hard training and had the right equipment. And so we too today have to have people to be trained in the capacity to scout ahead, to go in advance of the rest of mankind as pioneers into the future, so that they can bring back the knowledge and experience which will enable our planet to move forward into that future wisely and unitedly. The emphasis is on a team, and a team spirit.

I said, and this is something that is greatly to our comfort, that we are not acting blindly. And this is where the spiritual joins with our activities on the material plane. We can see in the past contemplations and illustrations of the future. I said yesterday that people speak of the Bible as if it were a book of religion. But in fact it is a book of the story of Man, from the first Garden to the ultimate City. In that context It offers guidance and predictions about man, so that we may go forward with confidence.

Let me give you a physical illustration taken from the story of the people of Israel. They started as slaves, and as slaves now emancipated they started the journey from Egypt to the Promised Land. And this is a parable, a parable of the story of mankind, which I wish to illustrate for you:

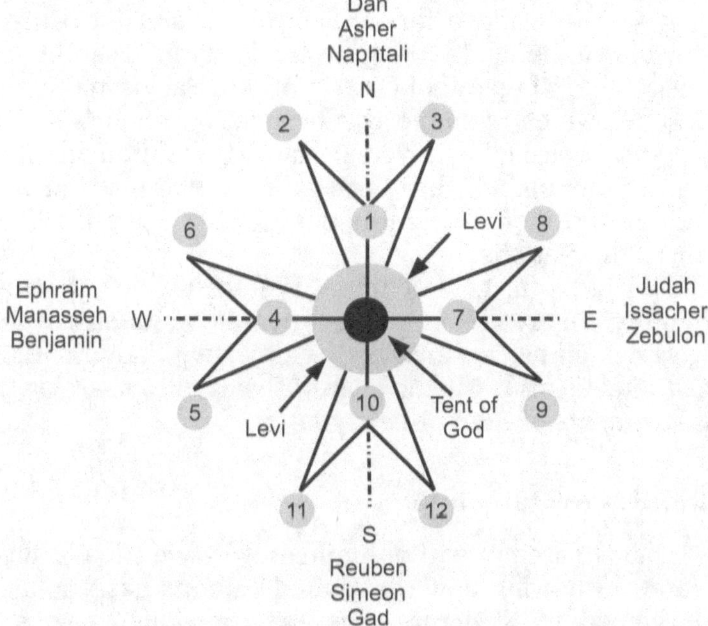

The pattern is given to us in the second chapter of the Book of Numbers. It is the pattern of World Community.

At the centre is the Tent of God, and in relation to it North, South, East and West, are the tents of the Twelve Tribes representing all nations. But one tribe has been taken away, the tribe of Levi, and to keep the number twelve another tribe has been subdivided. Joseph is replaced by his sons Ephraim and Manasseh. To Levi it was said that in the Promised Land, the ultimate world, this tribe would have no country of its own. It would be a priestly people, the instrument for communicating the mind of God to all the others as the Mediating Nation. Here we have in a symbolism more than 3000 years old the way in which the territorial nations would cooperate with each other through the medium-ship of a Servant-Nation having no territory.

I give you this illustration to show that in the providence of God we are not left without guidance and forced to discover a way for ourselves.

We have to move forward on our planet Earth from the international to the universal, symbolised by the ideal of the Kingdom of God, in order to achieve the purpose for which mankind was brought into being. And to help us towards the universal, towards the ultimate function of our planet, there has to be as the instrument a tiny minority of people functioning as a Servant-Nation for all the Nations.

So I bid you, take courage. We are not left to move blindly. We are able to move forward confidently in that work which has a much higher objective than any of us can imagine, but which we are privileged to share as the instruments of God. I thank you.

Replies to Questions

That we are not without guidance I have tried to illustrate by showing how the United Nations has gradually developed its structure from the previous League. It would very desirable that all permanent officials of the

United Nations should be world citizens, members of the Servant-Nation.

In ancient times people gave 10%, a tithe of their income, to God. So all nations should be willing to give to the service of mankind a tithe of their population. These individuals would represent the sense of the whole, and they should be willing to learn how to represent the whole, how to see things whole—that is with a spiritual eye. Nothing else will do. Individuals can know for themselves if they are called to this, and are willing to make the efforts involved in this and the sacrifices that are demanded. So now we have to begin as individuals to become world citizens, not as something vague and indefinite, but as something concrete and positive, a particular collectivity of persons.

A Jewish Gnostic

ELISHA BEN ABUYAH is one of the most intriguing personalities to be found in any literature. He was a learned man, a Rabbi, who in the prime of life had the courage to unlearn one of the most intricate and comprehensive systems of theology ever evolved by the ingenuity of man, in order to obtain empirical evidence of the Divine existence and activity. The difficulties of his self-imposed task as he faced them when the fires of youth were already extinguished would seem to have found expression in one of the very few of his sayings which have been preserved: "Elisha ben Abuyah said, 'If one learns as a child, what is it like? Like ink written on clean paper. If one learns as an old man, what is it like? Like ink written on blotted paper.'"[1]

There is always something awe-inspiring in the picture of a man of seemingly settled convictions, acknowledged a doctor of divinity, suddenly conscious of the futility of the way he has for so long taught, abandoning his former religious associations, and going out less than the least of all his pupils to seek a more satisfying faith.

Elisha ben Abuyah stands before us at the beginning of his quest, a dark figure of doubt against a background of divine radiance, daringly sacrilegious of artificial sanctities, careless of tradition, contemptuous of sophistry, challenging his people's God to reveal Himself unequivocally. We shall look in vain in the Rabbinical records for the real reasons which moved him to take the decisive step; of spurious reasons suggested by his adversaries to blacken his memory we shall discover plenty. The charges of loose living levelled against him by the Talmudic writers have proved so misleading that Dr. Max Letteris in rendering Goethe's Faust into Hebrew has used his name for that of the principal character. The

1 Aboth, iv 25.

"Faust of the Talmud" is no true description of Elisha ben Abuyah; rather is St. Paul, with whom he has frequently been compared. Like the great Apostle of the Gentiles, he had been educated "as touching the Law a Pharisee... touching the righteousness which is in the Law, blameless."[2] He, too, had seen a light in the way which completely changed the direction of his life: and he, too, as we shall see, had been "caught up into paradise, and had heard unspeakable words, which it is not possible for a man to utter."[3]

The animosity of the Rabbis against their errant confrere even extended to suppressing his name in almost every place where he is mentioned in the records. Instead of it they substituted the word Acher, which is Hebrew for "another." Some have thought that this expression was intended to distinguish Elisha ben Abuyah from Jesus, who is sometimes referred to under the disguise of Peloni "So-and-so," but this is entirely erroneous. Acher is an abbreviation of the colloquialism "dabar acher" (something else), or as we should put it "a horse of another colour."

Elisha ben Abuyah is nowhere mentioned in any contemporary document outside of the Rabbinical writings, and even in these he is mentioned but seldom. When we look up the references in the hope of discovering some biographical material or insight into his teaching we are very scantily rewarded. In almost every instance the notice is biased by theological animus, and even when this is not so, legends of a later date have coloured the passages, and we find ourselves with hardly any reliable data on which to build up a portrait of our subject. The best that we can do is to gather together the fragmentary remains and draw our own conclusions from them, bearing in mind the peculiar circumstances of the period. We have to face a position analogous to that of the Christian

2   Phil. iii. 5-6.
3   I. Cor. xii. 4.

Gnostics and the Church Fathers. Elisha ben Abuyah was a contemporary of Basilides; only Bishop Hippolytus, in his Philosephumena, has told us more about this great Gnostic teacher than both the Talmuds tell us about the Gnostic Rabbi.

But so little is generally known of Gnosticism in its specifically Jewish aspect that anything we can learn will help us to complete such theoretical impressions as we may have formed of this very remarkable divine philosophy.

The principal sources of information concerning Elisha ben Abuyah are the Palestinian and Babylonian Talmuds; the former concluded in the Fourth Century A.D. and the latter in the Fifth Century. While both Talmuds consist of commentaries on the Second Century Mishna (the Oral Law applying the Written Law of Moses to later conditions), a careful discrimination has to be made between their respective testimonies. If the Palestinian Talmud contains more folk-lore than the Babylonian, the Babylonian often suggests that recent conceptions were current at an earlier period than was actually the case.

The Talmud, it must be remembered, is a whole literature rather than a single book, and it is fortunate for our study, therefore, that nearly all the available material on the present subject is concentrated in a single chapter of this voluminous work—and that chapter acknowledged by all scholars to be the locus classicus of Gnosticism in the Talmud.

The Mishna on which the Talmud rests is divided into six sedarim, or orders, with an average of ten tractates to each. The second order is entitled Seder Mo'ed, on the Festivals, and its twelfth and last tractate is called Chagigah "Festival Offering." This treats of the duty of attending the three Pilgrim Feasts at Jerusalem, and the appropriate sacrifices to be brought on such occasions. The majority of the references to Elisha ben Abuyah are contained in the commentary on the second chapter of this tractate. The Mishnaic ordinance discussed, runs as follows:

"Men are not to expound unlawful unions with a company of three, nor the work of Creation with two, nor the Chariot with one; but if a man do so, he must be a wise man, and one who has much knowledge on his own account.
"Everyone who meddles with these four things that follow, it were better for him that he had not come into the world viz: what is Above, and what is Beneath; what is Before, and what is After. And everyone who does not revere the Glory of his Maker, it were better for him if he had not come into the world."

Those who are familiar with Jewish mysticism will be aware that it concerned itself with two branches of study —Cosmology and Theosophy. The first, called Ma'aseh Bereshith "The Work of Creation," found its inspiration in the first chapter of Genesis: the second, called Ma'aseh Merkhabah "The Work of the Chariot," sought to elucidate the mystery of the throne-chariot of God described in the first chapter of the book of Ezekiel. Of the two, the knowledge of the "Chariot" represented the higher degree of initiation. The Rabbis rightly discouraged mere idle curiosity in divine things, as it is said here, it were better for a man not to have been born than to meddle with the great mystery; what is Above, and what is Beneath; what is Before, and what is After. It was into the fellowship of this mystery "which from the beginning of the world hath been hid in God,"[4] that the author of the Epistle to the Ephesians declares that every sincere Christian can enter. "For this cause," he says, "I bow my knees unto the Father of our Lord Jesus Christ... that He would grant you, according to the riches of His Glory, to be strengthened with might in the inner man; that... ye may be able to

4 Eph. iii. 9.

comprehend with all saints what is the breadth, and length, and depth, and height... that ye might be filled with all the fulness of God."[5]

We have now to place the references to Elisha ben Abuyah in something like their proper sequence.

We know with certainty that he was born in Jerusalem before the destruction of A.D. 70. He was the son of a wealthy citizen, and was trained up to be a Rabbi. His later apostasy has been variously explained. On the one hand it is stated that this was due to his father having dedicated him to the study of the Torah from motives of personal aggrandisement rather than for the honour of God, and on the other hand to a pre-natal incident which is said to have taken place. According to this account, his mother when pregnant with him was one day passing an heretical place of worship, and was tempted to enter and eat of forbidden food (possibly the Christian Agapae) which infected the child with foreign ideas.

Elisha ben Abuyah seems to have been marked out for mystical pursuits, for Rabbinical adepts frequently met at his home. On one such occasion two scholars were engaged in discussion and became so deeply involved in their subject, that, forgetful of the presence of uninitiated persons they began to speak of the heavenly mysteries. Immediately flames began to play about them so that the father of Elisha exclaimed in alarm, "Do you mean to set my house on fire?'"

Elisha ben Abuyah made rapid progress in his divinity studies, and we may think of him as a young man learned in the Torah and found worthy to be initiated into the mysteries of the Creation and the Chariot. He was ordained a Rabbi and quickly rose to a position of authority, so that his judgment on difficult questions was greatly respected. His most famous pupil was Rabbi Meir, called the "Light of the Law," who remained devoted to him even after his rupture with orthodox Judaism.

5 Eph. iii. 9.

It is impossible with the limited and rather intractable material at our disposal to do more than suggest the reasons which led Elisha to give up his chair at the College, and go forth on a lone quest of his own. Did he come under the influence of some Gnostic sect? There is a curious statement that "Greek hymns ceased not from his mouth, and that often when he stood up to go out of the College heretical books which had been concealed in his clothing used to fall from his lap." We shall revert to this question a little later; but it is fairly certain that the Hadrianic war contributed greatly towards changing his opinions.

When the revolt of Bar Kochba, the pseudo-Messiah, was suppressed with difficulty by the legions of Hadrian in A.D. 135, the very harshest decrees were enacted against the defeated Jews. The keeping of Sabbaths and Festivals and the practice of circumcision were strictly forbidden. Scrolls of the Law were burned, the Colleges broken up, and the Rabbis prohibited from teaching on pain of death. Secret gatherings for worship and study were held in caves and desert places after the manner of the conventicles of the Scottish Covenanters. Elisha ben Abuyah was profoundly affected by the situation. We can discredit the accusation in the Palestinian Talmud that he was one of those who betrayed his companions to the Romans for trying to keep holy the Sabbath Day; but he is also accused of persuading the young scholars to forsake their study of the Torah and engage in some worldly occupation. The reason given is that he saw how a man loses his life in the performance of a precept for which God had promised the reward of length of days. Here perhaps is a tradition with a substratum of truth in it. Many a man's faith at a time of crisis has suffered shipwreck because of failure to discern God's justice in the affliction of the innocent. In our own day not a dozen years have elapsed since similar doubts were freely expressed by quite religious people. We know that several of Elisha's fellow Rabbis discussed most earnestly the text of Leviticus (xviii, 5) "Ye shall therefore keep my statutes, and my judgments: which if a man do, he shall live in them." "He shall live in them," they said, "not die in them." Finally, indeed, they publicly decreed that "Any sin denounced by the Law may be committed by a man if his life is threatened, except the sins of idolatry, adultery and murder."

We cannot entirely get rid of the evidence that for a time Elisha ben Abuyah gave himself up to a worldly life and altogether forsook his divinity studies. His sensitive mind had received a shock which may well have driven him temporarily to the other extreme, as sometimes happens with very highly strung individuals. While he was fighting the dark demon of doubt, his pupil Rabbi Meir would not leave him, and frequently urged him to give up the struggle against Providence and become conformable to the discipline of the Torah. Several passages of the Talmud concern themselves with this period of Elisha's history, and they suggest that he was very conscious of the enormity of his conduct. The passages are worth quoting for their revelation of the master's state of mind, and the deep attachment of his disciple.

"Acher (Elisha ben Abuyah) asked this question of R. Meir, after the former had gone forth into evil courses, and said to him, What is the meaning of the passage, 'God hath even made the one side by side with the other?' Meir replied. Everything which the Holy One, blessed be He, created. He created with its counterpart. He created mountains, He created hills, He created seas, He created rivers. Acher said to him, R. Akiba thy teacher did not say so, but he explained it as meaning that He created the righteous, He created sinners. He created the Garden of Eden, He created Gehenna..."

"There is a story about Acher, that he was once riding upon his horse on the Sabbath (an unlawful proceeding), and R. Meir was walking behind him to learn the Law from his mouth. Acher said to him,

*Meir, turn thee backwards, for I have already meas-
ured by my horse's hoofs up to this point the limit of
a Sabbath day's journey. Meir replied, Do thou also
turn thyself back. Acher said to him, Have I not
already said to thee, I have heard from behind the
curtain, "Return, O backsliding children, except
Acher." Meir forced him to enter a place of instruction. Acher said to one child, Repeat to me thy verse.
He said to him, 'There is no peace, saith the Lord,
unto the wicked.' He brought him into another synagogue. He said to a child, Repeat for me thy verse.
He said to him, "For though thou wash thee with lye,
and take thee much soap, yet thine iniquity is
marked before me."... He brought him into another
synagogue, until he had brought him to thirteen synagogues. They all repeated to him to the same effect.
In the last one (the child) said to him, 'But unto the
wicked (welarasha) God saith, What hast thou to do
to declare my statutes, etc.?' That child was a
stammerer. It sounded as if he had said to him, 'And
to Elisha (wele-elisha) saith God.' Some say that
there was a knife by his side, and that he was so in-
censed that he cut the boy in pieces and distributed
the parts among the thirteen synagogues; but others
say that he only said, If there had been a knife in my
hand, I would have cut him in pieces.*

The problem of God's justice, which so deeply concerned Elisha ben Abuyah, was intimately connected
with the more difficult problem of the Divine Nature. We
have noted that Elisha was accused of reading heretical
books in secret. Was he seeking through these a solution
to the Great Mystery? Perhaps the first of the passages
just quoted may furnish a clue. Why should Elisha ben
Abuyah be interested in the text "God also hath set the
one over against the other "? When we compare the
reason given on the authority of R. Akiba, we are reminded of the teaching of the Graeco-Ebionite Clem-
entine Homilies. There the Apostle Peter discusses the

justice of God, and puts forward the theory of pairs and opposites.

"But if anyone," says Peter, "according to the opinion of this Simon the Samaritan, will not admit that God is just, to whom then can anyone ascribe justice, or the possibility of it? For if the Root of All have it not, there is every necessity to think that it must be impossible to find it in human nature, which is, as it were, the fruit. And if it is to be found in man, how much more in God! But if righteousness can be found nowhere, neither in God nor in man, then neither can unrighteousness. But there is such a thing as righteousness, for unrighteousness takes its name from the existence of righteousness; for it is called unrighteousness, when righteousness is compared with it, and it is found to be opposite to it. Hence, therefore God, teaching men with respect to the truth of existing things, being Himself One, has distinguished all principles into pairs and opposites, Himself being One and sole God from the beginning, having made heaven and earth, day and night, light and fire (sic), sun and moon, life and death.... And if pious men had understood this mystery, they would never have gone astray...."[6]

Here we are in contact with a definite teaching of the Gnostic schools, which in its non-Jewish form was sometimes associated with a dualistic conception of the Deity. Were the books which Elisha read Gnostic works? Possibly Christian-Gnostic documents. Rabbi Meir, the disciple of Elisha, was acquainted with and made a bitter word-play on the Evangelion (Gospel); Aven-gilyon "idolatrous-revelation" he called it. And we are reminded that Trypho the Jew of Justin Martyr's Dialogue, who was confessedly a refugee from the Hadrianic war, says "I am aware that your precepts in the so-called Evangelion are

6 Clem. Hom., ch. xv

so wonderful and so great, that I suspect no one can keep them; for I have carefully read them."[7] This Evangelion was one of the books of the Minim (the Talmudic term for sectaries who were deists), and of the many passages in the Talmud where encounters with the Minim are referred to, the subject of discussion is frequently as to whether there are two Powers in heaven.

Had Elisha ben Abuyah any leanings towards the doctrine of the Two Powers? In order to answer this question we must now quote the most famous passage concerning him; that of the four sages who entered Paradise in ecstatic vision.

"Our Rabbis have taught four men entered Paradise; Ben Azzai, Ben Zoma, Acher and Rabbi Akiba. R. Akiba said to them, When you approach the stones of pure marble, do not say, Water, water! for it is said, 'He that speaketh falsehood shall not be established before mine eyes.' Ben Azzai gazed and died. Concerning him Scripture says: 'Precious in the sight of the Lord is the death of his saints.' Ben Zoma gazed and went mad, and concerning him Scripture says: 'Hast thou found honey? Eat so much as is good for thee.' Acher cut the plants. R. Akiba departed in peace"

The Babylonian Talmud comments:

"'Acher cut the plants'—He saw Metatron (the Angel of the Presence) to whom is given permission to sit and record the merits of Israel. Acher said, We are taught that in heaven there is no sitting down, nor anger, nor lack, nor weariness. Are there—God forbid! —two First Principles? They brought out Metatron and gave him sixty strokes with a lash of fire. They said to him, Why, when thou sawst him (i. e., Elisha), didst thou not rise up? He was given permission to strike out the merits of Acher."

7 Dial. c. Tryph. ch. x.

Unfortunately for this commentary the Metatron idea was not current among the Jews so early as the time of Elisha ben Abuyah; yet the dualistic inference is much the same. "Acher cut the plants." Those who have studied Jewish mysticism will know that a distinction was made between two heavenly orders of beings, the Netiyoth (plants)—those who are of the Divine Essence and yet have a distinct existence like the branches of a plant, and the Nephridim (separate ones)—such as the ministering angels who have no Essential connection with the Deity. Elisha's error consisted in cutting the plants i.e., in assuming the separate existence of two co-equal Deities, instead of merely distinct Intelligences in the one Essence of the same Deity.

Of the later life of Elisha ben Abuyah tradition tells us nothing. So much is clear, that he was a married man, that he lived longer than the Psalmist's span, and that he was never reconciled to orthodoxy. There is a hint that he died at Rome; but this is unlikely.

The last word of the Talmud is a tardy acknowledgment of the greatness of a learned but wayward teacher.

"When Acher died, they said 'Let him not be brought into judgment, but let him not be admitted to the world to come.' Let him not be brought into judgment, because he studied the Law; but let him not be admitted to the world to come, because he sinned. R. Meir said, 'It were good to bring him to judgment, but also to admit him to the world to come. Would that I might die, that I might cause smoke to ascend from his grave.' When R. Meir died, smoke ascended from the grave of Acher. R. Jochanan said, 'A mighty deed it was to consign his teacher to the flames. There was one among us, and we found not a way to deliver him. If I take him by the hand, who will snatch him away from me.' He also said, 'Would that I might die, and extinguish the smoke from his grave.' When R. Jochanan died, the smoke ceased

from the grave of Acher. The public mourner uttered this expression over him, 'Even the keeper of the door of Gehenna stood not his ground before thee, O our teacher'."

"A daughter of Acher came to Rabbi. She said to him, 'Rabbi, give me some food.' He said to her, 'Whose daughter art thou?' She said to him, 'I am the daughter of Acher.' He said to her, 'Is there still of his seed in the world? And yet it is written, He shall have neither son nor son's son among his people, nor any remaining where he sojourned.' She said to him, 'Remember his study of the Law, and remember not his deeds.' Immediately there came down fire, and consumed the seat of Rabbi. Rabbi wept and said, 'And if those who disgrace themselves through the Law are honoured thus, how much more those who obtain praise through their use of it?'"

From an article in "The Occult Review", February 1931 Volume 53.

Holocaust and Us

(An Address by Hugh J. Schonfield, Geneva, 22 August 1979)

First of all, I would like to thank Mrs Payro and Mlle Valensin for arranging this occasion, then to thank all of you who have come to take part in this subject, I must confess to you that when I was invited to come and speak on "Holocaust and Us", I had very great qualms as to my capacity to contribute anything useful to the subject, and I felt the burden of responsibility very greatly as regards the slaughter of some 6 million Jews under the Nazis. I only viewed this from a distance. I met people who had escaped, I met people who had been in the concentration camps and had got out ultimately with their lives, but that was not the same thing as being intimately involved in what after all was one of the most terrible events that have happened in human history.

I have to come to this subject from another angle, the angle that speaks to us all, that belongs to the history of the human race. But the more what they call civilization has advanced, the more it has become practicable for inhumanity to take more positive and terrible forms than it could do before. And it has meant, when we think of that Nazi period, and of the propaganda of that period, which after all was the cause and the justification if you like, for the steps of the so-called "Final Solution". When we look at that, we can see something that has been with the human race for a long time past and which seemed here to come to a great climax. But a climax portending what? And this, I think, is something with which also we need to concern ourselves. And so it turned quite inoffensive names into names of horror, like Auschwitz, and Belsen, and Buchenwald, and Dachau, names which have come to signify some great aberration of the human spirit which overflows in a wave of evil which has been difficult for many to understand. If I may come to something very simple, at this point, we often form groups and societies of one kind or another and when we do this we often see written into the prospect of the group that this body has come into existence without discrimination of race, class or creed. Somehow, these three terms seem to represent, or sum up, the most difficult forms of association that humanity has had, about which there has been conflict and war and suffering at all times in the area of Race in the ethnical side, of Class on the political side and of Creed on the theological side. These three expressions of human relationships have seen those which have caused perhaps the greatest sufferings, the greatest bloodshed, the greatest violence. And yet, each of them has something in itself which is of worth.

Going back in time, perhaps I could express this in one word: that the difficulty which humanity has always experienced is something related to what we can call OTHERNESS, something that is different from what we are to which we have to adjust or relate in the best way we can. And in that association, we have found from time immemorial-it did not start with antisemitism—it started far back in the history of the human race, with one tribe facing another, and within tribes and groups finding people who seemed to be different, the hunchback, the idiot, all kinds of persons who seemed at variance with the life of the group, and whom it seemed to be the objective of the group to eliminate.

I remember, some of you with classical remembrances will also remember, that great sage who lived near the time of Jesus, Apollonius of Tyana, who had to get rid of the plague at a particular city he visited; and he determined that this plague was embodied in a blind beggar, whom the town's people proceeded immediately to drive out and to destroy. And we have similar references in the letters of the Apostle Paul. For those of you who know your New Testament, he speaks of the followers of Jesus as being "the off-scouring of all things until this day".

Referring to an ancient custom among the Greeks again whereby when a great calamity threatened, they used to try and pick up the worst people they knew in the town and literally cast them into the sea, to drown, in order to avert this calamity. We know about the evil eye and all these superstitions that turn very ugly ladies into witches, and so forth. This has been something that has been a legacy of time in the history of the human race, this difficulty of absorbing otherness. And when we go back to the Bible again, and begin to take in the story of the Hebrews, this crops up continually. On the way to the Promised Land, the heathen king is made to send his prophet Balaam to curse that alien body that has arrived in their region. But the prophet was defeated and said:

"How can I curse those whom God has blessed?"

Much later, we find a little book, the Book of Esther, in which we have again the suggestion made to the Persian monarch of a great Empire that there is among you a people which has different ways from other peoples and which has different laws and do not keep the king's laws. And so the decree goes forth that this people is to be eliminated and massacred on a given day.

And when Jesus taught, he gave us the Sermon on the Mount, as that collection of his sayings is called, where he was speaking as a Jew to fellow-Jews, and he was telling them that they needed to be different from the people round about them, that it was not good enough if they only loved their brethren: any Gentile did that. You had to do something more, you had to love the alien and even the enemies, those who are hostile to you. You had to reverse the judgment of history, and take in and accept that which the ordinary life of man condemned and flung away and would destroy.

I don't know if you know that the 53rd Chapter of Isaiah has been interpreted in Christianity as the reflection of someone treated in this kind of outcast fashion, and it

has been applied to Jesus. But it has also been applied to
the Jewish people themselves. The figure Is there, the
one who grows up as a root out of dry ground. There is
no beauty in him that we should desire him. Look at the
Nazi caricatures, the great hooked nose, the fleshy lips of
the caricature of the Jew. He is held in front of the
people as one whom we are not to desire. "He was despised and rejected by men, a man of sorrows, and acquainted with grief, and we hid as it were our faces from
him. But it was only our sorrows, and our grief, that he
was carrying himself." That is a very apt picture of the
Jew in history in his relations with the world around
him. We, as I have said, think in terms of trying to destroy otherness, not recognizing in fact what benefits otherness can confer upon us. And so we always look for
what we call the scapegoat, the one who can rid us of our
problems, our frustrations, our inabilities, and take that
burden away. And the more we can find something ugly,
or something which we can describe in hostile and op-
probrious terms, so much the more are we willing to load
our burden on this caricature of reality. We find that the
ancient image of evil is the devil, this black creature, as
ugly and as grotesque as anyone could depict him in order to present to our eyes something so alien, so beastly,
so inimical, that we would readily run from him in an
opposite direction. But you see, this kind of attitude
brings also an attitude of enmity to an extent that people
become blinded and cannot see even their fellow-men in
a true light.

It was long before Hitler, that antisemitism raised its
head in Europe. And those who went in the name of
Christ to rescue the Holy Sepulchre from the Saracens
crossed Europe with their troops, the crusaders and
their following, and on their way massacring, every Jew
they could find. Why should they wait till they got to the
Holy Land to begin the good work? It could start very
much sooner. It could start on your own doorstep. And
so right across Europe the story of death and torture fol-

lowed the advent of an aim which in its own ideals had everything to speak for it. And yet, what in fact it accomplished was that there was held before the eyes of the people that here are the killers of Christ, here are the deicides. And the cry rang out, "Hep! Hep!" Whenever there was an attack on the Jewish Community. This "Hep" is believed to derive from "Hierosolyma est perdita", Jerusalem is destroyed, and was identified with the destruction of the Jewish people as having been the instrument of the death of Jesus.

Now, take this thinking: and see where it leads you, right throughout the period we call the Diaspora or dispersion. We have this phenomenon of this people, with its different ideology, with its separateness, moving mile by mile, kilometer by kilometre if you like, stretching out throughout the world. It is described as the dispersions but in fact it was not really that, and it was due a universalist idea that it happened, because it really began with a very famous man in history, Alexander the Great, who set out on world conquest, and indeed created a vast Empire from Europe to India, in very few years. He came to Jerusalem on his way, and he was greatly impressed by what he found there. And so, one of his acts of statesmanship was to say: "Let us try and think not in terms of 'otherness', but in terns of relationship under one system of government with common ideals." Then, he saw in the Jews a leaven which, if it were extended through all the countries, could be the unifying influence in the world. And so, he invited Jewish people to settle in all parts of his Empire, One quarter of the new city he built in Egypt, Alexandria, was a Jewish quarter; and he had Jews serve with him in his march towards the East. So there began to be an understanding, as a result of this dispersion, that somehow into the world at large there had crept insensibly almost a type of personality which was unique in the sense that it was universalist in its outlook, which taught the exist-

ence of God and Father of all Mankind, which taught
that there was a future in which the whole of Mankind
would subscribe to faith in that One Being and would
become united and at peace under His Laws. We have a
passage in the prophet Zachariah: "in those days, ten
men—that is a religious quorum for worship among the
Jews—ten men out of all nations of the Earth will take
hold of the robe of a Jew and say 'We will go with you
because we have heard that God is with you'.

This strange intrusion into the world at large of this
strange people was a phenomenon of OTHERNESS
which it was extremely hard to swallow and digest. And
it did create an atmosphere of tension, an atmosphere in
which there was a great deal of persecution of these
people who had come into these different lands. We have
many accounts of those persecutions and the difficulties
they involved.

And so, you come right on from there into the atmosphere of the modern world. And the climax of this ideal
comes in the development of what modern political and
social and ideological theory has enunciated.

Just for a moment lingering with the ancient past, we
have the story, that the Hebrews themselves tell of how
things had broken up in the world so that it had ceased
to be unified. The breakup due to human ambition. The
Jews saw the Great Powers warring around them, rather
like Switzerland being surrounded with such Great
Powers. There was Assyria, and Babylon and Egypt:
Great Powers warring with one another warring with one
another. And these people, philosophizing on this said
that it was ambition, ambition on the part of these countries, which had reached such a height of impiety that
they sought power at all cost, even the cost of storming
heaven. They saw Ziggurat temples in Mesopotamia,
they saw the pyramids in Egypt, And these were the
towers which man in his own strength was erecting up to
        contend with the majesty of God, At that time,
said the chronicler, everybody was of one speech, and

consequently they all understood one another, and therefore peace reigned. But with this ambition came the fall. And the very very word "Babel" has signified that to us, when we use the word "babble" today, and mock the now "bar" (barbarian) whose tongue is alien to us. And so by confounding the speech of these ambitious peoples all the evils, said the chronicler, had come about.

One day, perhaps, the world will again be of one speech, and perhaps then again unified. It was certainly a Jew who had thought of that, not so very long ago, Zamenhof, when he invented the language of Esperanto.

And so, in the modern world, with this great capacity, a capacity far exceeding the ancient powers of the past, the idea of race was brought under Nazism once again to the fore, as indeed on the Eastern side the idea of class was brought to the fore under Communism. And so the Nazis enunciated this idea of the purity of race—something that had already been heralded by philosophers in the past, men like Professor Miller in the 19th century, Nietzsche, and so on, the idea that certain people (and this is of course quite the opposite of the Hebrew idea) that certain people were destined for power, to exercise power over others, over other races, over other peoples. And to this end, the idea of a universalism must be contested. And the Jews were the expression of it. And so, in the propaganda that the Nazis gave out, they attacked the Jews as what they described as Cosmopolitan. We cannot have Cosmopolitanism, because Cosmopolitan means World Citizen, and a world citizen outlook. In other words, you cannot have an element in the country which has a world loyalty, loyalty to a world ideal. And the only way in which you can assert your own position must be to destroy that element which undermines the whole idea of dictatorship and authoritarianism and domination. We are meeting elements of it still in the attacks in the East, the eastern block of Europe, on the dissidents, the people who think beyond the narrow confines of the viewpoint of the State, who cannot be assimilated, and who believe in breaking down the barriers which it is to the interest of Great Powers to maintain.

And we are getting it in all kinds of contexts, in modern racialism, whether you say "Black is beautiful" or whatever it may be. But certainly no one has dictated it. And this is a fact surely of scientific note. We see creatures who are accustomed to the conditions, of a particular climate, the fox which will wear brown fur in the summer and a white fur in the winter. And so with the human race it has extended around the globe over many thousands of years, living under particular climatic conditions. And as a consequence we have these colour changes. But there is nothing that dictates that the West should be Caucasian or Nordic. There is nothing that dictates that the Middle-East should be brown, or that Africa should be black, or that Asia, Far-East or Asia should be yellow. The world belongs to all the families on the Earth and we should accept that. With the new development of travel, of scientific advance which gives us freedom of communication and movement with a rapidity which we have never had before, with new satellites relaying messages from every direction and pictures of what is going on, all this means that the whole question of these three things, RACE, CLASS, CREED, is coming up for judgment now in a new way. We have to look at them with new eyes, and we have to terminate this idea that a person of another race is something OTHER, or that a person of another colour is something OTHER. We have to come to the recognition that we have to reach back to the idea of recognizing all as our fellow's and our brother's, and that otherness is to be received, to be welcomed, and to be enjoyed as part of the great pattern of the planet. And similarly, in our ideas of class, this again has to be upheld, the understanding that we are not to divide our into segments by certain political or economic classifications or description of occupations. Nor are we to take in our religions a viewpoint which harbours a perpetual hostility towards a different interpretation of the riddle of the universe which we are trying to expound for ourselves as we slowly climb along the ladder of evolution.

So now, perhaps, the Holocaust may have done something of tremendous value and worth that sacrifice, that profound sacrifice of those millions could have meaning, and have done something of tremendous value, IF OUT OF THIS we are willing to learn, willing to love our brethren as ourselves, in the old term, while recognizing our sense of new responsibility for every part of humanity, a new sense of the worth of every being, so that people are not there to be slaughtered and tortured at the will of any body of persons in authority.

We have seen the evil consequences around us of that Holocaust in Germany, only too many of them. When we look at what has been happening in the Far-East we are shocked at the sufferings Boat People as we call them, who have escaped in these battered ships to some hopeful haven. We are getting too narrow, we are getting too insular and the danger, you see, on that account, the danger is that we shall have not learnt this lesson, and to the contrary we shall be carrying the evil forward more and more, so that our sense of the worth of our fellows becomes less and less in our eyes, and that we regard everything as expendable which does not suit our convenience or our narrow limitations.

And now we have the other side. WE CAN move forward into the idea of a KINGDOM OF GOD ON EARTH. WE CAN move forward into a relationship where we are prepared to learn from the past, and to learn from many expressions of past faith, some of which I have quoted to you, and say: "Here and now we begin to MAKE THE WORLD ONE by being at one with it in ourselves". And suddenly no longer is there a stranger and a foreigner, but a fellow-citizen, one of the saints, one of the family of God, which after all is ALL humanity, and which in the Hebrew ideal which was challenged by the Holocaust, was one which saw that possibility ahead as the goal and the aim of history, that we were to move forward into a time when these differences, these distinctions, these animosities, these hatreds would end in a new burst of love and understanding.

Now, we look for people, YOU and YoU and YOU, we look for people who will pin their lives to that kind of vision, and conduct themselves on the basis that" I am part of this humanity, I have RESPONSIBILITY to that humanity. When I meet with OTHERNESS, I shall not despise it, 1 shall approach it and seek to relate to it and to understand it, and to recognize that it is part of the scheme of things." And as a consequence of this, there will come up like a shoot out of dry ground this new personality which is prepared to bear the sorrows of the World and to take upon it its sufferings, because it has found in itself the Love with which to do it.

You may say, "This is utopian idealism". I believe it is practicable. Because individuals have done this, it can be done on a much greater scale, first by the few but ultimately by multitudes, and eventually mankind at large, will discover the unity in diversity So, when I am moved to speak about the "Holocaust and Us", this is the only way in which I can respond.'

Christ Against Caesar

I am a historian, and my lecture is on a dramatic historical subject—Christ Against Caesar. But before I address myself to it, it is essential that I should explain the nature of the historical. History is a recording of life experiences, whether of persons, groups or nations. Sometimes these experiences are very ordinary and unemotional. Sometimes they are very exciting and even sensational. The human tendency is to adorn and embellish the more emotional and significant by attributing them to mysterious and unearthly causes, thus making them larger than life. The fact, however, is that exactly the same factors are at work in dull every-day affairs as in very unusual ones. There are no forces which intervene only sometimes, on special occasions.

I may illustrate the circumstances out of personal experience. I was Barmitzvah just before the outbreak of what was later called the First World War. At the time war on this scale was a novelty, and it was the first - because of modern invention—to be fought not only on land and sea, but in the air and under the sea. Spiritual factors and prophetic fulfillments were inevitably introduced. This was Armageddon, the final contest between the forces of good and evil. Troops in the trenches saw the vision of the Angels of Mons. As a Sign of the Times the Holy Land was to be freed from the Turks. The British General Allenby had his name construed as Allahnebi (Prophet of God in Arabic). There was the exotic figure of Lawrence of Arabia. It was even put forward that a passage in the Great Pyramid of Egypt foretold the march of events in detail. My father Major William Schonfield recruited the Jewish battalions which fought under Allenby for the liberation of Jerusalem. I was present in London at the official celebration of the Balfour Declaration. Christians seized on the news that at long last the Jews were to return to their own land.

Consequently the Second Advent of Christ must be imminent. Human imagination would not be thwarted of its convictions.

And here I must go back to the dawn of history. Primitive man was to discover in himself a sense of purpose and a capacity to plan for desired ends, and he was to discern that everything around him, near and far, was functional. He deduced, therefore, that behind and beyond everything there was objectivity, and that this must be governed by higher powers than himself, powers with intention and immortality. This consciousness was the birth of religion.

But there was another development, both individual and collective. This was a consciousness of being under guidance, of being chosen for a special purpose. Sensitives would see in events the evidences of such choice, and consequently would invest them with signs and wonders in confirmation of their significance.

I am not representing such experiences as proof that the affirmations of various religions are purely human interpretations of the nature of reality, and in effect are gilding the lily. But the historical approach does witness to human readiness to overplay and adorn what it regards from a spiritual viewpoint as significant. And this tendency runs readily to invention to make alleged happenings more impressive, more supernatural. Where we can we have to get behind what is put under our noses, and particularly we have to take into account that most of the time nothing remarkable is happening at all.

In the story of Jesus nothing is more telling as proof of his total humanity than the fact that for some three quarters of his life not a single miracle is associated with him. When the Christian Church elevated him to deity the obstacle of what are called the Silent Years was appreciated, and Infancy Gospels were created which related the wonders and magical acts Jesus had performed as a boy.

In another context, the story of Israel, a mature conviction of having been entrusted with a divine mission to mankind stimulated by prophets and seers was enhanced by investing the origins and early history of the nation with signs and wonders, notably in the description of the Exodus from Egypt. And it is significant that in the Book of Exodus in the Bible the people of Israel is called God's firstborn son.

Historically there is a very positive relationship between Jesus and Israel in the context of their sense of choice and destiny. Jesus could not have been the one he believed himself to be if he had not credited to the full the choice and destiny of his nation.

To get to the root of the matter we have to go back in time to the return of the Jews from the Babylonian Exile. The influence of this experience was very great. Contact with the Babylonian religion, and more impressively and acceptably with Persian Mithraism, left its mark both on Judaism and on Jewish ideology. There began to be recognised an ascending series of heavens and spiritual hierarchies, while on earth it was accepted that time was divided into a series of Ages. In these Ages the forces of Good and Evil were in contention, the Children of Light warring with the Children of Darkness. The final and crowning Age would witness the triumph or Light, the ultimate rule of God on earth, in which the righteous believers would participate by resurrection.

In the Book: of Daniel the Children of Light are depicted as homo sapiens, the Son of Man, while the warring Empires of the world are likened to brute Beasts. This Son of Man is brought before the Ancient of Days and receives a kingdom that will never pass away. But there has been another change. The seers no longer think of all Israel as the Chosen People, but only of the righteous in Israel. It is the Saints of the Most High who possess the Kingdom.

It has been conceived that Israel was not to be like other peoples.

It was to be the intermediary between God and Mankind and the means of communicating God's will to the world. The prophets saw the Promised Land as a Holy Land. All nations would send their delegations to it to learn the Laws of God and the ways of peace. In the latter days Israel would have become a Kingdom of Priests and a Holy Nation.

But this was not the state of affairs in the time of the kings of Israel and Judah. There was idolatry, apostasy and evil-doing, which the prophets denounced, and in those days was born the doctrine of the Faithful Remnant, the persecuted and suffering Servant of God. The, disloyal would be punished by captivity and exile, which could be anticipated because Israel was the natural battleground of contending Great Powers, Assyrians, Babylonians and Egyptians.

The seers anticipated the appearance of successive savage beast imperialisms before the new world order of the Kingdom of God could manifest itself, the Son of Man era. History presented one such imperialism in the Syro-Greeks under Antiochus Epiphanes when the Temple at Jerusalem was desecrated and the attempt was made totally to destroy the Jewish Faith. The circumstances had called for the Resistance Movement of the Maccabees and the creation of a new body of Jewish pietists the Chasidim, forerunners of the Essenes.

The Messianic Hope was now more positively taking shape in its conception of two ideal 'anointed ones', a high priest and a king (the two Sons of Oil), who would be instrumental in welding together the Elect of Israel of the Last Times. The Chasidim because of the initiative of their priestly leader, now known to us from the Dead Sea Scrolls, and because of the priestly status of the Maccabees, emphasised the Priestly Messiah, while other pietists like the Pharisees stressed the advent of a Royal Messiah of the line of David, but agreed that his forerunner would be a priest, identified with the return of the Prophet Elijah, whom they claimed had been a priest.

Here matters stood when what was identified by the pious as the fourth and worst of the Beast Imperialisms came on the scene. Less than sixty years before the birth of Jesus one Roman General Pompey, intervened in Jewish affairs, and even dared to enter the Holy of Holies in the Temple at Jerusalem. From then on the Romans exercised a growing influence, and they were the power behind the Idumean tyrant monarch Herod the Great, who got rid of the Hasmoneans and turned Palestine into a Police State,. On his death Augustus Caesar took over as executor of Herod's will. Soon he deposed Herod's vicious and incompetent son Archelaus, and Israel's homeland was virtually annexed to the Roman Empire as part of the province of Syria. Judaea was governed by a Roman procurator. But even areas like Galilee, still nominally under Herodian rulership, now had the Roman capitation tax levied on their inhabitants.

This evoked, especially among the sturdy northerners, a resistance movement, headed by Judas of Galilee, who raised the standard of revolt under the banner "No Ruler but God", and which required to be bloodily repressed by Quirinius, the Roman governor of Syria. The whole country was now in a sorry state, with Jewish victims on Roman crosses visible across the land and multitudes held in prison. Spies and informers abounded. The country was riddled with fear of what was being experienced and what might still be pending. Nerve cases were multiplied, the blind, the dumb, epileptics and paralytics. No wonder many were convinced that these must be the Last Times, and that now, if ever, a Deliverer must come.

Among those who set their hopes on Deliverance was a Jewish artisan called Joseph, himself a descendant of the Davidic royal house. It may be significant that he gave his firstborn son the name Joshua (in Greek Jesus) after the hero of old who had led Israel into the Promised Land. In those days there were known descendants of King David still living, and they were given a special function in the service of the Temple at Jerusalem.

There is as yet no certainty when Jesus was born. One Gospel record claims that it was in the lifetime of King Herod, about 6 BCE, while another makes it when Quirinius was Syrian governor, around 6 CE. By then the circumstances of the birth of Jesus had become legendary and impossible to verify, since these Gospels were written after the devastating Jewish War with the Romans (67-70 CE).

Jesus was the eldest of a large family. He had four younger brothers and at least two sisters. This much is clear. And on the evidence they were settled in Galilee and lost their father while Jesus was still a young man. Jesus adored Joseph, who - it may be inferred - filled his young mind with the Messianic Hope, not excluding the information that it could be his own branch of the Davidic family which would provide the Deliverer. What are called the Silent Years in the life of Jesus could be very eloquent if in them, as seems most likely, he had sought to discover from exponents of the Bible, including the Essenes, what would be required of the Messiah, what would be his activities and fate. He could well have encountered itinerant Essene prognosticators, as even King Herod had done as a young man. The main function of the Messiah was twofold, first to reach all in Israel who would constitute the Elect of the Last Times, and second to deliver his people from the power of the Romans. Subsequently he would overthrow the Roman Empire, and Inaugurate the ultimate era of the Kingdom of God on earth. But the victory would not be by force of arms, but by the exhibition of special qualities. The Messiah himself would undergo much suffering, and even appear to incur death.

Here not only was it the interpretation of the Hebrew Bible which had to provide the required information, not only the Psalms of David but also contemporary expositions and works like the Dead Sea Scrolls, the Testaments of the XII Patriarchs, the Psalms of Solomon, the Assumption of Moses, etc.

Because of the obsession that the Last Times of the old world order had arrived there was an outpouring of apocalyptic literature. We have to involve ourselves in this atmosphere if we are to understand how Jesus came to be convinced that he was the awaited Messiah. The conviction became a certainty when suddenly there appeared on the banks of the Jordan the eerie figure of John the Baptist, garbed like one of the prophets of old. Here surely was Elijah reincarnated.

We cannot be sure what age Jesus was at this time. He could well have been approaching thirty-five. For many years he had been the family breadwinner while his brothers and sisters were growing up. It was only in full maturity that he could achieve a sufficient measure of freedom.

But in all this time his mind had been at work, defining his Messianic function, weighing up the manner in which he would have to proceed. He had a keen intelligence and powers of observation, and was fully aware of what he would be up against. Claiming to be the Messiah meant claiming to be King of the Jews, and to do so without the authority of the Roman Government would be committing an act of high treason against Caesar for which the punishment was death. He would be arrested and killed when his mission had hardly begun. And if he did not announce himself as the Messiah how could he win the support of his people and bring many of them to repentance?

The answer to that question was solved by John the Baptist. He was calling Israel to repentance by announcing that the Kingdom of God on earth was at hand, and dipping them in the Jordan as they confessed their sins. Jesus had to encounter this Elijah figure, and take up his proclamation. His Messianic mission had begun. We are told that he went into the wilderness to sort things out, and rejected that he could achieve his ends by signs and wonders. It was the real world, the social and political world with which he would have to contend. This meant that for the first part of his mission he must not disclose himself as the Messiah, and must take every precaution to avoid arrest.

Prudence dictated that Jesus should embark on his enterprise in patriotic Galilee, the home of the Jewish freedom movement. The first whom he called to him as proclaimers of the Kingdom of God were fishermen from the lake, the Sea of Galilee. They were physically strong Jewish loyalists, and their possession of boats secured for Jesus a line of escape across the water to other territory. Finally, Jesus selected twelve immediate disciples, symbolic of the Twelve Tribes of Israel. Some of them belonged to the Zealot movement. Later he would send them throughout the country to preach repentance to the lost sheep of Israel.

Naturally, Jesus could not deny that he was the Messiah, even if he could not yet claim it. He therefore shrewdly spoke of himself as the Son of Man, a Messianic term only employed by the Jewish mystics, which would convey nothing to the Jewish public or to the Romans and their agents.

But even the proclamation of the coming Kingdom of God had its dangers because of its political implications. At this time John the Baptist had been arrested by the ruler of Galilee, Herod Antipas and thrown into a dungeon in the fortress of Machaerus. Wherever Jewish crowds gathered spies and informers were present. Cleverly, therefore, Jesus spoke of the coming Kingdom in parables, always concluding with the words: "Let him who can catch my meaning do so". But now things were hotting up. The chosen envoys returned with word of their general lack of success, and Jesus himself found his proclamation of the Kingdom fall largely on deaf ears. He was greatly distressed, and denounced the little towns where his message had been delivered. If Jesus was to win his people it was time for new tactics, much more positive and dangerous tactics. Preparation had to be made in the south. It was customary for Jesus, like other Jews, to make the pilgrimage to Jerusalem for the festivals of Passover, Pentecost and Tabernacles, and he had good friends—some eminent ones—in and around the capital.

In a Gospel partly reflecting the memoirs of an eminent Jewish follower in the south we learn that towards the end of his activities, after the festival of Tabernacles Jesus stayed on in and around Jerusalem for several months making his preparations. It is intimated elsewhere that before this Jesus had already disclosed his Messianic identity to the Twelve; but he did not keep them with him at Jerusalem, and had warned them not to reveal his status as king. Caution was of the utmost necessity because the antisemitic Pontius Pilate was now the Roman governor of Judea.

Jesus knew well what he was up against, and he had already given evidence of being a brilliant tactician. Now he surpassed himself. We can follow his devices as they came into operation, and they particularly affected a young follower in Jerusalem called John, commonly known to us as the beloved disciple; but others were also involved. The die was cast. Knowing the consequences Jesus was now going to acknowledge his kingship.

He rejoined his followers in the north, and soon with them and the Galilean pilgrims he was on his way to Jerusalem for the Passover. Near Jericho, we are told, a blind beggar called out to Jesus, "Pity me, Son of David!" Until now, when anyone had addressed him in public as Messiah, Jesus had silenced them. This time he did not do so.

As the pilgrims neared Bethany, close to Jerusalem, Jesus sent two of his disciples ahead, telling them that they would find a young ass tethered at the entrance to the village, and they were to bring it to him. Arrangements had clearly been made with the friends of Jesus at Bethany. The disciples of his were keyed up, expecting him to reveal himself openly as Messiah. Now they saw the fulfilment of the prediction of the Prophet Zechariah.

"Rejoice, daughter of Zion, your king is coming to you riding upon an ass." At once the cry was raised, "the prophecy is fulfilled. Jesus is our king. He has mounted on his ass. Hosanna, Son of David!"

There was no turning back now. Jesus had boldly and publicly committed himself. He had accepted the plaudits of the Galilean pilgrims as the rightful ruler of Israel. And by so doing he had deliberately made himself guilty of treason against Caesar, and in a clever manner. The Romans were familiar with the bands of Jewish pilgrims coming to Jerusalem for the festivals uttering glad cries and chanting their Hebrew songs, and the troops were under orders not to interfere.

But now Jesus had to provoke against himself the Sadducean chief priests, members of the government subservient to Pontius Pilate, but fearing and hating him. These aristocrats materially profited from the Temple market, where foreign currency was exchanged, and commonly called after the previous high priest, 'Annas' Bazaar'. Jesus both gained the support of the Jewish populace and assured himself of the enmity of the chief priests by overturning the tables of the moneychangers. "It is written," he cried, "My house shall be a house of prayer for all nations; but you have turned it into a den of thieves."

Other incidents followed, attempts to discredit Jesus with the Jewish masses. He was asked, "Should we pay the Roman poll-tax to Caesar?." Jesus replied, "Show me a denarius". It bore the inscription "Tiberius Caesar Divi" (divine Caesar). Brilliantly, he said, "Give Caesar what belongs to him," and he paused. "But give God what is God's." From this time, however, Jesus prudently did not spend a night in Jerusalem where he might have been assassinated. He always returned to Bethany, to the company of his friends, and this was a Jewish pilgrim reception area, where he would be safe.

And now he was particularly involving one of his chosen Twelve in his plans, the former freedom-fighter

Judas. How he was worked upon we cannot now know. But very clearly, and at the appropriate time, it was the intention of Jesus that he should be betrayed to the authorities, and consequently suffer on a Roman cross. He would suffer as King of the Jews as an act of atonement for his people's sins; but also he would triumph over death to bring the Roman Empire to an end, and substitute for it the era of world peace and justice known as the Kingdom of God.

We have to enter very closely into the mind of Jesus, as he now brought into effect what I have called THE PASSOVER PLOT. This required the cooperation of several notable persons with whom Jesus had made arrangements quite unknown to his Galilean associates. To avoid the risk of violence when many Jewish lives would be lost, Jesus had to see to it that he would not be arrested either in Jerusalem or in Bethany. Yet he had to keep the Passover in Jerusalem, and he would do so at the house of the high-placed disciple John. The Twelve, including Judas, could not be allowed to know this prematurely. But there was a garden near the city at Gethsemane, which Jesus favoured, and where he meant to be found at the appropriate time. This of course was known to Judas.

How cautious Jesus was can be judged by the devices he employed. When he was asked where in the city he would hold the Passover seder, he told two of the Twelve to go there. At a certain spot they would encounter a man carrying a water-pot. This man would lead them to a house, where they were to ask which was the arranged room for the service. They would be shown an upstairs room where they would prepare. There was no give away of the address of the house. But the records convey later that it was on the Ophel, on the east of the city.

We take up our story again with the arrest of Jesus in the Garden of the Civil Guard under the authority of the Sanhedrin, accompanied by some of the servants of the chief priests. It is said that Peter followed discreetly to the court of the high priest's palace. When Jesus was interrogated he admitted that he was the Messiah, and had therefore committed a crime against Caesar. He had committed no crime in Jewish law. Therefore as early as possible the next morning Jesus was brought before the governor Pontius Pilate on a political charge, rebellion against Rome.

Pilate had every reason to be extremely suspicious that this was a move by the chief priests to discredit him. But he had no alternative as Rome's representative than to examine the prisoner, who was a most unlikely looking rebel leader. Jesus sealed his own fate by insisting he was king of the Jews, and was condemned to be crucified. The Jewish people, of course, had no hand in the matter, one of court intrigue, and had no knowledge even that Jesus had been arrested. It had been in the dead of night, when they were in bed in their own homes.

But the planning of Jesus was far from finished. Had it not been predicted in the Psalms of David: "You will not leave my soul in the grave, neither will you suffer your holy one to see corruption. You will show me the path of life."? To complete the Messianic programme he must escape death. Normally, death from crucifixion did not occur quickly. It was intended to be a long drawn-out torture. Jesus had therefore to cut the experience very short, and had made sure of this in his advance planning. The device he chose was a simple one, to have a drug administered to him by an onlooker to render him unconscious. We are told that he called out, "I thirst", and then someone unknown raised a soaked sponge to his lips, and shortly after he was apparently dead. It would seem that Jesus had concerted this, and other plans, with Jewish friends in the government when he was in Jerusalem some four months previously. One of them was Joseph of Arimathaea, who had had a tomb made for himself not far from the place where executions took place, at Golgotha. Joseph was now at hand, as soon as Jesus lost consciousness, to go as a man of authority to Pilate and claim his body. We are told that Pilate was amazed, as well he might be, that Jesus should have died so quickly, but having received verification he granted Joseph's request. The plan was essential, because it assured that Jesus would be placed in a tomb above ground, whereas no revival would have been possible if he had had his body dumped in a pit and covered with soil, which is what would have happened to the two men crucified with Jesus.

The plan had great risks, but it was carried out in faith. Jesus would rest unconscious in the ventilated tomb over the Sabbath, and then be taken out in the night. Essenes, who were skilled healers, would be at hand to take charge of him, and when he was sufficiently recovered he would rejoin his followers in Galilee.

But there was a contingency which had not been anticipated. A zealous Roman soldier had plunged a spear into the side of Jesus when he was taken down from the cross. It was too late for any change of plan, and Joseph of Arimathea and his friends could only hope. As soon as possible on Saturday night the tomb was entered: it could only be opened from outside by rolling aside the great circular stone which covered the entrance. The body of Jesus was removed in haste, leaving the tomb wide open, since the stone was not rolled back to close it.

When women of Jesus' company came there early on Sunday morning this is what they found. Greatly shocked and troubled one of them, Mary Magdala, ran back to Jerusalem to tell his followers, "They have taken away the Master, and we don't know where they have put him."

We have a recollection that one of the Essenes, who dressed in white, had been left at the tomb to tell the followers of Jesus that he was no longer there, but would be reunited with them in Galilee. In the records created many years later he appears as an angel, and there are various elaborations arising from the belief that Jesus had been raised from the dead and had temporarily ascended to heaven. Without such a conviction the Messianic movement which would develop into the Christian religion would never have got off the ground. The inexplicably empty tomb was very strong evidence. The records do not explain the sudden disappearance of Joseph of Arimathea from the scene; but legend has it that he fled to Britain.

Like Moses, the body of Jesus rests somewhere in Israel, and in the words of the Bible "no man knows the place of his burial to this day." No one more sincerely and honestly sought to fulfil what was expected of the Messiah; and in the strange way things work out he was to triumph in Rome, having conquered the Caesars.

Jesus showed that there is another way to overcome your enemies than by violence, and that with total dedication you can make an important dream come true.

The Truth About the Deity of Christ

The doctrine of the Deity of Christ, not to be confused with the eventual doctrine of the Trinity, was a development resulting from the fall of Jerusalem in AD 70. The Jewish War with the Romans had the effect of severing Christianity from its Jewish roots, so that it now became predominantly represented by Christians of various pagan origins in different parts of the Ro-man Empire. It was understood from available information that Jesus had appeared as King of the Jews, a term which for Gentiles implied a status of deity as the son of a god. It was an ancient belief that rulers were divine incarnations, and it had come strongly to the fore in the Graeco-Roman world. The Ptolemies in Egypt be-came sons of the god Ra, and the Caesars found it politic to claim deity as sons of Jupiter. Temples were erected for their worship and that of the goddess Roma.

An inscription in the reign of Augustus has been found dating from 7 BC, in which he is hailed as "Caesar, who reigns over the seas and continents, Jupiter, who holds from Jupiter his father, the title of Liberator, Master of Europe and Asia, Star of all Greece, who lifts himself up with the glory of great Jupiter, Saviour."

But it was later emperors who would stress their deity, and notably, near the end of the first century AD, the Emperor Domitian, who insisted that he be addressed as "Our Lord and God Domitian" (Suetonius, Lives of the Caesars, Domitian xiii). There is an echo in the Fourth Gospel, where Thomas addresses the risen Christ as "my Lord and my God" (Jn. xx, 28). This Gospel dates from the beginning of the second century. Early in the same Gospel we find Nathanael exclaiming to Jesus, "Rabbi, thou art the Son of God; thou art the King of Israel"(i. 49).

Earlier books for Gentile Christian consumption were more careful. Luke, for example, only has it that Jesus "would be called Son of God", not that he would be Son of God (Lk. 1. 35). And just before, verse 32, the word "called" is also used, the emphasis being on the words "the Lord God shall give unto him the throne of his father David, and he shall reign over the house of Jacob for ever." In other words Luke is stressing that Jesus would not be divine like pagan rulers, even though as King of Israel he would bear the Son of God title. And we should note that it is "the Lord God" who confers this honour, the undivided Deity. In the Acts similarly the protomartyr Stephen has a vision of Jesus "standing on the right hand of God" as the Messianic Son of Man (vii. 55-56).

It is evident that for the first Christians what was significant about Jesus was his descent from King David, which qualified him to be the Messiah (the Christ). Hence the need for the genealogies in the Gospels of Matthew and Luke. No question of the deity of Jesus arose; which might have been the case if he had been born elsewhere than in Israel. Obviously, what required to be investigated was, in what sense the term Son of God could be applied to Jesus without implying deity.

If we can ascertain this from the Bible an age old problem which has divided Christians from the Jews would be substantially resolved. When we study the Bible we find the expression Son of God used in a variety of contexts, none of them relating to the Being of God Himself. We find it applied to a category of non-terrestrial beings with human attributes, as in the Book of Job (i) and in Genesis (vi. 2). It is applied to Jewish monarchs such as David and Solomon, and in the New Testament to Adam (Lk. iii. 38). But very consequentially, as we shall be considering shortly, it is applied to the People of Israel. Jesus commonly referred to himself as the Son of Man. This was a term in the Book of Daniel relating to the People of God, which by the time of Jesus had given rise to a mysterious Heav enly Messiah, but not God who would come to Earth in the Last Times, represented in the Book of Enoch. Jesus used this description of himself advisedly, since though it had Messianic significance it was very little known even to the Jewish people (Jn. xii. 34).

To claim to be the Messiah (the Christ) was a claim to be the rightful and ultimate Jewish king, and under the Roman government such a claim was illegal and the penalty for it death, unless the claimant had the authorization of Caesar and the Senate. If Jesus had declared himself to be the Messiah at the commencement of his activities, as John claims, he would not have lasted very long.

The other Gospels are right that Jesus only admitted that he was the Messiah at the very end of his ministry, first to his disciples privately and then publicly by riding into Jerusalem to the plaudits of his fol-lowers as king of the Jews. He knew well then what he was do-ing and what the outcome must be. It was under Roman Law that he was crucified for the crime of declaring himself king of the Jews. Throughout his public activities Jesus had had to be extraordinarily circumspect, resorting to parables when speaking to the crowds on the topic of the coming Kingdom of God, because of spies and informers. He remained in Galilee most of the time, because it was not under direct Roman rule, only indirect, and the populace was highly patriotic, Jesus was safer there than anywhere else; but even John the Baptist had been got rid of. So skill and caution was imperative.

With the Land of Israel an occupied country by an alien pagan Power these were dangerous days. Unfortunately, Christian expositors dwell very little on the political circumstances. They are too caught up in theology. It is much that uniquely is in the Fourth Gospel that is most out of line with reality, and contradicts the other Gospels. Its Jesus does not even speak as a Jew or in a Hebrew idiom. He refers to the Law of Moses as "your Law" (x. 34), when naturally he would say "our Law" or "God's Law", and asserts that all who preceded him were thieves and robbers (x. 8). In fact, very largely, the Jesus of the Fourth Gospel wears the likeness of the author of the Epistles of John. And significantly, Gentile Christians find this much more acceptable and reliable.

Those elements in the New Testament—and there are many—which are of a 'Jewish' nature are rarely quoted or expounded. John the Elder of Asia Minor, who flourished early in the second century AD, has much to answer for, utilising for his purposes the reminiscences of the Beloved Disciple when they suited him. The tombs of both were at Ephesus. The Son of God reference which we have held over is the key to its employment for Jesus, and it is rarely if ever cited by Christian theologians. It is found in Exodus (iv. 22) where God tells Moses to say to Pharaoh, "Israel is My Son, My Firstborn... Let My Son go that he may serve Me" (cp. Jer. xxxi. 9, Hos. xi. 1). The whole burden of the Bible is that the people of Israel was chosen by God as Messiah Collective for the nations, to be itself a Kingdom of Priests and a Holy Nation, to bless all peoples and lead them to the worship of One God and in the ways of peace and righteousness.

It was because Israel was far removed from these functions that it was predicted that an Anointed King (Messiah-Christ) would come to recall them to their mis-sion. This king would be Son of God by adoption as was Israel (Ps. ii). Jesus, descended from King David, apprehended his Messiahship in this sense, claiming that he had only been sent to the lost sheep of the House of Israel, and telling his envoys to go to no one else.

Thus Jesus as Christ, the ultimate Jewish king, was not Deity incarnate, but had a relationship with God as his mentor and inspirer in a paternalistic manner. For a Jewish king to accept that he was divine like pagan rulers was a grievous sin (Acts xii. 22-23). If Jesus had committed it he could not possibly have been the Christ. According to the Jewish followers of Jesus in the first century, as certified by the Hebrew Gospel they used, Jesus had received the Messiahship not at birth but at his baptism, when a voice from heaven declared, "Thou art my beloved son, in thee I am well-pleased" and "I have this day begotten thee." The same reading is found in Codex D, and the Old Latin version, taken from Psalm ii. 7.

This rules out any antecedent divinity of Jesus, and fully explains why he should immediately after have been driven into the wilderness to be tempted by Satan in his new Messianic capacity. The problem for the Church is that it clings to its Heathen rather than its Jewish antecedents, completely forgetful of the teaching of the Apostle Paul, who insisted that all Gentiles who gave their allegiance to Jesus became thereby naturalised Israelites (Rom. xi and Eph. ii. 11-15).

Gospel Untruth

A Disclosure of Christian Fraud

Introduction

The contentions of this essay are so consequential that it calls for an introduction which is substantially autobiographical. It is, to say the least, unusual for a Jew to be so involved in the beginnings of Christianity as I have been in my writings and researches throughout a long life. There has seemed to be in this a kind of fate which there was no evading, and it began to manifest itself in my childhood.

I am a Londoner. My father was an orthodox British Jew who had come south from Glasgow in the late nineteenth century to seek his fortune, and married my mother, who came from an Anglo-Jewish family which had settled in Cornwall in the reign of Queen Anne. I was their second son, born at the opening of the twentieth century, in May 1901.

Christianity was on our doorstep, since there was a church at the corner of our road, and as a child I wondered about what were the beliefs of those who attended. But indeed it was even closer, because, strange as it may seem, in our dining room there was a very large oil painting, and its theme was Peter denying Christ after his arrest. How we acquired it I have no idea. While the picture did not raise a problem, something else did, the question of my elder brother and myself attending synagogue wearing our school caps which bore the emblem of a cross. We were then at Colet Court, preparatory school for St. Paul's Public School. Actual contact with Christianity only began when I entered the senior school on the Classical side shortly after the outbreak of the First World War. I had a master who was also an

Anglican clergyman, and who spoke to me of Jesus as "our Saviour and your Messiah". I had not previously thought about the Messianic, and my interest was aroused.

The Great War, as we called it, the First World War, was now in progress, on land and sea and in the air, creating an apocalyptic atmosphere, so that many believed it heralded the Second Advent of Christ. There was the Vision of the Angels of Mons, and the rescue of the Holy Land from the Turks. The British General concerned, General Allenby, had his name interpreted in Arabic as Allah-nebi (Prophet of God). His forces included Jewish battalions. My father, Major William Schonfield, was in charge of recruiting them, and my elder brother was one of those who joined, and was wounded on the road to Jerusalem. There was the amazing Balfour Declaration, declaring that the British Government favoured the restoration of Palestine as the National Home of the Jewish People. I was present at the great Jewish Meeting in London to mark the event.

I left school to go on Land Work, and was recommended to a farm by a gentleman who believed that we were living in the Last Times and they had all been mapped out in the passages of the Great Pyramid of Egypt.

On the farm were conscientious objectors to military service, members of the sect of Christadelphians.

Inevitably there were discussions about the Messiahship of Jesus, and as a consequence I borrowed an English Bible from my landlady and read the New Testament for the first time. It made a deep impression on me, convincing me that Jesus had believed himself to be the ultimate king of the Jews his people were awaiting. What was unacceptable was the Christian doctrine of his deity, and I felt sure that it had been the conversion of pagan Gentiles which had been responsible for this development. I wanted to know what had been the convictions of his Jewish followers, not fully represented in the New Testament. There had once been a Hebrew Gospel, of which only significant fragments had survived in quotations. I was given an incentive in my quest when a second-hand bookseller opposite the British Museum notified me of an ancient Hebrew version of the Gospel of Matthew, which I acquired and translated into English.

The path was set for me to become deeply involved in Christian Beginnings, and the significance of the Messiahship for Jesus himself.

Few Christians, because of their pagan tradition which dwelt on his deity, have given much consideration to what it meant for Jesus to believe himself to be the ultimate king of the Jews, their final leader in a time of Roman domination. Here was a man who could say to his immediate followers: "You shall sit on twelve thrones judging the twelve tribes of Israel."

It may be quite a new idea to the reader to think of Jesus as a Jewish patriot. But he must have been one if he was convinced that he was the chosen descendant of King David to deliver his people from their enemies and inaugurate the promised era of Peace and Righteousness foretold by the Prophets.

As a youngster, growing up in the atmosphere of the First World War, I was strongly patriotic myself, and when circumstances brought me in close contact with Christians it registered that Jesus had claimed to be king of the Jews. We Jews had a monarchy of our own. My studies and researches were increasingly concentrated on Christian Beginnings, while holding down a job in Public Relations and Advertising. My approach was not that of a theologian. I had always been a keen student of history. My concern was to get behind the New Testament, to all the circumstances of the period before the Jewish War with the Romans of 67-70 AD. Inevitably, this brought me in close contact with the Works of Josephus, and it was necessitated that I should make a fresh translation of the New Testament from the Greek on literary and historical lines. All written after the War, how much of historical reality did this represent? I had to gain understanding of Paul's convictions, the Jewish Apostle to the Gentiles who had never known Jesus personally and was a deep-seated mystic. I had to pursue Gospel origins, and especially to recognise the historical Intentions of Luke-Acts and the Jewish-Gentile complexity of the Johannine literature nurtured in Asia-Minor.

Step by step my researches moved forward over several decades, greatly stimulated by discoveries such as that of the Dead Sea Scrolls and the Sayings of Jesus from Egypt.

Familiar as I now was with ancient religious literature, my approach was inevitably academic rather than theological. I could not think of the Bible as the Word of God, as orthodox Christians do, since all literature of whatever kind was created by humans for human purposes. From ancient times each religion had its sacred book or books, for which exalted claims were made, and their presentations were in contradiction of one another, proving their human contrivance. For academics in the Biblical sphere there was knowledge of the Apocrypha and Pseudepigrapha, Jewish works such as that of Tobit, the Enoch literature, Baruch, and the Testaments of the XII Patriarchs. How many ordinary Christians are familiar with these? But the Early Church thought of them as authoritative. So, in the case of the Testaments, they inserted predictions of Jesus. Here are some examples.

"For our father Israel is pure from the transgressions of the chief priests [who shall lay their hands on the Saviour of the World]" Test. Levi xiv. 2.

"And after these things shall a star arise to you from Jacob in peace, and a man shall arise like the sun of righteousness, walking with the sons of men in peace and righteousness. [And no sin shall be found in him. And the heavens shall be opened unto him, to pour out the Spirit, even the blessing of the Holy Father: and he shall pour out the Spirit of Grace upon you.]" Test. Judah xxiv. 1-3.

Similarly we may take the Sibylline Oracles, regarded as divinely inspired by the Romans, where Christians inserted a prediction of Jesus.

"And one chief man shall come again from the sky, who stretched forth his hands upon the fruitful tree, the best of the Hebrews, who once shall stay the sun in its course, calling upon it with fair speech and holy words" Siby. Orac. Bk. V. 256-259. "Shall stay the sun," is of course a reference to Joshue (i.e. Jesus).

Such allusions could be multiplied, and they advise us that the New Testament Gospels are human contrivances and were not composed as Divinely inspired. In various places these documents flatly contradict one another.

Quite naturally and quite properly, therefore, my investigation of the New Testament was conducted with the employment of the same kind of criteria as would be used in relation to other works recovered from the past, such as the Dead Sea Scrolls. The idea of Divine Inspiration did not enter into the matter. Some outstanding Christian scholars have acted in the same manner. There has been an almost total separation of archaeology from theology. But Christian divines have been handicapped by their inadequate familiarity with the Jewishness of Jesus, so that they could sufficiently embrace the political aspects of the Messianic. They have also been reluctant to lower the prestige of the Gospels, such as Luke and John, to which my researches have been particularly directed.

Different religions have different sacred books which often in their teachings contradict one another. Similarly in the New Testament there are radical differences between the Gospels, which if they were divinely inspired would be impossible.

Christians use what they call the Holy Bible, composed of Old and New Testaments, and claim it as the

Word of God. But the documents themselves clearly distinguish between material attributed to Divine inspiration and secular records. Thus in the Old Testament we have the Ten Commandments ascribed to God and the instruction given to Moses and the Prophets, while in the New Testament the Revelation is said to have been given by God to Jesus. But all the rest of the Biblical material makes no claim to Divine authority, and consequently it cannot be objected to to investigate it critically in the same manner as any non-Biblical or secular documents which have reached us from antiquity.

This principle applies also to manuscript variations, interpolations and copyists' errors. The verbal inspiration of the Bible is a nonsense, and even more so—as I have encountered—the verbal inspiration of the English King James, or Authorised, Version, which has been responsible for much false doctrine.

I was very much involved in such matters when it became essential for me to edit and translate the New Testament records from the Greek (the Authentic New Testament). It will suffice if I give one instance of how a copyist's error may easily occur. This is found in Phillipians i. 21, where the text reads: "For me to live is Christ, and to die is gain." The scribe, whether by accident or intention, has changed the word chrestos (useful) to Christos (Christ). What Paul had actually said was: "it is useful to me to live, and an advantage to die. But if I am to live physically it means an effort on my part, and I hardly know which to choose. I am in a quandary between the two."

Once one was relieved of the incubus of Divine inspiration in dealing with the New Testament documents it became practicable to investigate them more systematically, especially those which professed to relate to historical circumstances. In this book Luke-Acts especially, and then the Gospel of John, have been singled out for illuminating treatment.

Gospel Beginnings

The Gospels in the New Testament are the outcome of an endeavour to convey to Gentiles an account of Jesus of Galilee in the role of Jewish Messiah (Christ in Greek). Such a task was far from easy, even when such Gentiles had embraced monotheism and had some understanding of the Jewish Bible. The advent of the ultimate king of the Jews to deliver his nation from its enemies could not be expected to enlist the enthusiasm of non-Jews. What Gentiles needed was a personal delivery from sin and death by means of a substitute victim of superhuman status. Accordingly the Glad Tidings for Jews had to be fashioned by Christian missionaries to Gentile requirements, more especially after the disastrous Jewish War with the Romans in 67-70 A.D.

Early Jewish-Christian teaching had made much of the fulfilment in Jesus, and his experiences, of passages in the Jewish Bible to which they were held prophetically to relate. This activity in itself inevitably produced a basic catalogue of biographical circumstances and events; so that in fairly broad outline, and in some detail, they could be followed in sequence. Of course, such an activity could also have another consequence, the invention of events deemed to be required by prophetic intimation.

Apostolic emphasis had naturally been on circumstances which would demonstrate to Jews that Jesus had been the awaited Messiah. But for Gentile audiences it was Jesus as a man that mattered. What kind of man had he been? What had he said and done? What had been his earthly experiences?

When Peter had gone over to the proclamation of Jesus to Gentiles, who were not even on the fringe of Judaism, he was in demand because he had been so close to Jesus and could relate his personal reminiscences. It is on record that Mark acted as Peter's interpreter, since Peter was at home in his native Galilean Aramaic. Subsequently, Mark had employed these reminiscences to compose a Jesus-Story, the nearest thing to a biography, though the order of events could not be certain. This would serve as a basis for much of the compositions of Matthew and Luke. which stress the activities of Jesus in Galilee. Mark has no Nativity story or any account of the appearances of Jesus after his death. It is well-known to scholars that the present ending of Mark's Gospel was added much later.

The writing of other Gospels was an outcome of two factors. One, of course, was that the original Apostles and even their immediate hearers were dying out. The other was the failure of the Second Advent to materialise as anticipated. There were not a few who were asking, "What has become of the promise of his advent, for since the fathers fell asleep everything goes on exactly as it has done since the beginning of Creation" (2 Pet. iii. 4). Since the destruction of Jerusalem and the Temple in 70 A. D. there had been no sensational development.

The consequence was that many Christian communities in different countries were out of contact with each other, and some were beginning to be affected in their beliefs and practices by local non-Christian ideas and institutions. If this went on it would not be long before there would be a variety of Christianities, some of them almost a complete reversion to paganism.

There was the pressing need for a selection, representative of the north, south, east and west of the Roman Empire respectively, a selection which would incorporate the most favoured expressions of the Jesus-Story. This selection in the second century A.D. began to be regarded as Divinely inspired, and with the Letters of Paul gave rise to a second part of the Bible, described as the New Testament (New Covenant). In fact, however, only one book in the resultant New Testament actually claims Divine inspiration. This is the book of Revelation, which opens with the words: "The Revelation of Jesus Christ, which God gave him to show to his servants what must shortly transpire. So he made It known by communicating it through his angel to his servant John, who in turn gave out God's Message and the testimony of Jesus Christ."

It is highly significant and important here that when the Revelation was set down there was no attribution of deity to Jesus: he Is clearly distinguished from God. That doctrine only began to take over around the dawn of the second century A. D., and it was partly influenced by the insistence of the Roman Emperor Domitian (81-96 A.D.) on his own deity. This was especially in the last few years of his reign.

We have every entitlement to approach the canonical Gospels as human compositions, not Divinely inspired, which they make no claim to be, and consequently to investigate how each one of them originated. As regards Luke, one of the two we are investigating, the Gospel is introduced by a Foreword in which the author claims that his Work is the outcome of his personal research of the circumstances. No claim whatever is made to Divine inspiration. We are fully entitled to treat the canonical Gospels, and those which are uncanonical, as purely human compositions, and accordingly to quest for the derivations and intentions of the several authors.

From a biographical angle the reminiscences of Peter had been almost unique. Other members of the Twelve may have related things in the course of their propaganda activities; but they are not on record.

The activities of Jesus were predominantly in Galilee. Consequently the Synoptic Gospels have very little to tell us of the experience of Jesus in Judea until the finale. Naturally, as a good Jew, he goes to Jerusalem for the three Pilgrim Festivals, Passover, Pentecost and Tabernacles. But that is all. And even before his crucifixion at Jerusalem he advises his disciples that when he has risen (i.e. from the dead) he will go ahead of them to Galilee, a purpose which in Matthew is subsequently confirmed by an angel (Mt. xxviii. 5-7). In this tradition there was something of a resentment of the Galileans against the Judeans which was typical of the northerners.

We are not allowed to know that Jesus had important friends in the south, notably Martha of Bethany with her sister Mary and brother Lazarus, of whom we are told in John's Gospel. Mark and Matthew make no mention of them, and Luke refers to them without indication that they were Judeans. They just live "in a certain village" which could be anywhere.

When it comes to the Last Supper, and Jesus is to celebrate the Passover in Jerusalem, it is evident from the Synoptic Gospels that he has privately - unknown to the Twelve - made prior arrangements with the owner of the house. He would need to have been a close and indeed intimate friend of Jesus to be ready to harbour this man whom the authorities were seeking. We are told of the precautions that were taken, but not of the householder's identity. But if we study the Fourth Gospel, which uniquely covers the activities of Jesus in the South, we can discover that the owner of the house in Jerusalem was in fact John, "the Dear Disciple" as he describes himself, who rightly had a chief place, leaning on the breast of Jesus, at the ritual feast.

Without John's Gospel a vital part of the Jesus-Story would be missing. But It is by no means easy to get at, as our investigation will disclose, because that Gospel was taken over by a Greek Christian also called John, who was responsible for the long quite uncharacteristic speeches of Jesus set down in it. This man gives his Gentile identity away when he makes Jesus speak to the Jews of "your Law" (x. 34), when of course as a Jew Jesus would have said "our Law". We are able to identify him with John the Presbyter, author of the three Epistles of John in the New Testament. Of the "Dear Disciple" Eusebius the fourth century Christian historian cites a letter from Polycrates bishop of Ephesus to Victor of Rome that this John had been a Jewish priest, indeed a high priest, who had worn the sacred breastplate (Euseb. Eccles. Hist. Bk. V. ch. xxiv).

This, however, is a bit far-fetched. Certainly the Dear Disciple was a priest or belonged to a priestly family. He was known to or related to the high priest Annas (Jn. xviii. 15), and was able to get Peter admitted to the high priest's palace where Jesus was being interrogated. Since he had a house in Jerusalem he was able to offer a home there to the mother of Jesus (Jn. xix. 27), and this house was the first Christian meeting-place.

Apocryphal Gospels were devised in the names of some of them; but their fraudulence is very obvious. A great hiatus had been created by the circumstances of the Jewish War with the Romans for which Christian scholars insufficiently allow. In that War (67-70 A.D.) Galilee had suffered terribly at the hands of the Roman forces, and it had been chiefly in Galilee that the activities of Jesus had been pursued. There can have been few individuals left, now sixty years old and more, who had heard or encountered Jesus. We have to accept that when the so-called Synoptic Gospels were published, especially Matthew and Luke early in the second century A.D., there had to be considerable resort to invention. Such invention was partly governed by the location in which a particular Gospel was written.

Matthew is significant because it represents the infant Jesus as being given refuge in Egypt, land of the Mother Goddess Isis with the infant Horus in her arms, the country to which so many Jews also fled from the Roman forces. To assist him, the author of Matthew would readily have had access to the Gospel of Mark, since according to Christian tradition, as reported by Eusebius and others, Mark had travelled to Alexandria from Italy bringing his Gospel with him.

Tradition also ascribes to Matthew a compilation in Hebrew of the utterances (logia) of Jesus, which could have embraced such material as is represented in the Gospel by the Sermon on the Mount. But even so we are still left in Matthew with a substantial folklore element and misunderstanding of Hebraic elements, so that we must not think of the author as being the apostle.

The lateness of the composition of Matthew is Indicated at the close. There, when the body of Jesus is found missing from his tomb, the guards who were supposed to keep watch over it, are instructed to say, "His disciples came by night and stole him while we slept," The note is then added, "And this is the version that is still current among the Jews." These words are the real ending of the Gospel. But the strong Hebraic texture of much of its material did not permit of its reception into a Gentile Christian Canon without correction. There had to be something to qualify the statement made in It by Jesus to his Apostles (x. 5-6), "Keep away from Gentile centres, and do not enter any Samaritan town. Go instead to the lost sheep of the house of Israel."

Accordingly, a postscript had to be added to this Gospel where the resurrected Jesus is made to tell the eleven disciples, "I have received complete authority in heaven and earth. Go, therefore, and make disciples of all the Gentiles, immersing them in the name of the Father, and the Son, and the Holy Spirit, teaching them to observe whatever I have commanded you. I shall indeed be constantly at your side until the Consummation of the Age."

Anyone who reads the Gospels with an open mind cannot fall to see how they contradict one another in material particulars. And this is notably true of the chronology. Matthew, for instance, claims that Jesus was born in the reign of King Herod, who died in 4 B.C., while Luke claims that it was when the Romans conducted a census of the Jews while Quirinius was legate of Syria (6-7 A.D.). Christian scholarship has failed to reconcile this contradiction. Matthew also claims that Joseph and Mary only settled in Galilee after the birth of Jesus, while Luke states that Joseph and Mary lived in Galilee but travelled to Bethlehem of Judea because of the census, which required registration at the ancestral town (in this case of King David), and thus Jesus was born there. In the Synoptic Gospels at the close of his public life, and immediately before the Passover, Jesus attacks the merchants at the Temple in Jerusalem. In John's Gospel this incident is placed at the very beginning of his activities (Jn. 11. 13-17).

Such discrepancies, while unfortunate, can be understood when account is taken of the gulf between the events related and the time when the Gospels record them. Not only were none of the Gospels written in Galilee or Judea; they were written some 75 to 100 years after what is related, and in the intervening period Galilee and Judea had been devastated by the Jewish War with the Romans. It is the subsequent treatment of these documents as Holy Writ, Divinely inspired, which has given them a false authenticity.

Only one of the Four, Luke, makes the claim in his Foreword: "Since it is the case that many have endeavoured to draw up an account of those matters held by us to be fact, exactly as they transmitted them to us who were initially the eyewitnesses and bearers of the Message, I have thought fit myself, as I have conducted a thorough investigation of all the circumstances from their beginnings, to set them down for you consecutively, most excellent Theophilus, that you may apprehend how well-founded are the things of which you have been informed." We shall be investigating the reliability of this statement.

One of those to whom Luke would be alluding would be the author of Mark. And Mark's Gospel, as I have pointed out, comes the nearest to an authentic account of Jesus, as embodying the recollections of Peter. There is much less of the miraculous in it, and Jesus is much more of a healer.

Of the four Gospels in the New Testament those that make major claims to be authoritative are Luke, as a record of historical facts, and John, as the presentation of a superhuman Christ. It is to test and challenge the validity of these claims that this book will address itself.

Gospel Truth and Untruth

A Literary and Historical Investigation of the Jesus Story

Starting Point

Christianity as a religion is a blend of Judaism with Paganism. Initially the word that the awaited King Messiah had appeared in the person of Jesus son of Joseph, descended from King David, was communicated solely to Jews, as was appropriate, and almost entirely to inhabitants of Judea and Galilee. But the extension of coverage was inevitable, to embrace the Jews throughout the Diaspora (substantially the Roman Empire). There was not an immediate initiative to send Jewish emissaries from Jerusalem. This came later. But from all over the Empire Jews came to Jerusalem for the three pilgrim festivals of Passover, Pentecost and Tabernacles, and in Jerusalem synagogues were provided to meet their linguistic and accommodation needs.

In the natural course of things, as any sensible person will agree, Jews from abroad would learn that a body had come into being in Israel claiming a certain Jesus as the awaited Messiah. His followers were being quite vociferous about it. Report would be bound to spread to other areas as Jewish pilgrims to Jerusalem travelled back to the lands in which they lived. And with this development there would come another. The Synagogues of the Diaspora were attended not only by Jews, but also by Gentile Unitarians, attracted by the simplicity of Jewish belief and worship. Thus without any set purpose or design rumours and reports about the Messianic development in Judea would begin to get through to non-Jews, and arouse their interest, especially in the social, political and religious atmosphere of the Roman Empire in the middle of the first century AD.

The Messianic had nothing to do with theology, except in so far as it proclaimed one unseen God and Father of mankind. It was an ideology expounded in the Pentateuch and by the Hebrew Prophets. This affirmed that the People of Israel had been chosen to be a priestly people on behalf of all peoples, giving out God's laws to mankind, and by this means leading them in the ways of Peace and Justice. The failure of Israel to live up to its calling, by indulging in idolatry and wanting to be no different from all other nations in its political policies, led to a further development. This now called for 'anointed ones' (Messiahs), ideal kings and high priests, to bring the nation back to the acceptance of its ideological function. The political Messiah (Christ in Greek) would be a descendant of David, who would call Israel to repentance and rescue the nation from its enemies.

As a result the Messianic objective would be fulfilled, and the world would be converted to the ways of peace and justice in the Kingdom of God on Earth.

All nations would come to Zion to worship God and learn the ways of living together in harmony. There would be a thousand years of ideal existence, and many in the time of Jesus believed that those in the past who had led saintly lives would be resurrected from the dead to share in the Golden Age. The followers of Jesus as the Messiah no less believed that after being raised from the dead he himself had been taken to Heaven, from whence he would speedily return to our world as am immortal being and the millennial ruler under God, having put all enemies under his feet.

The religion of Judaism was inseparable from the Biblical plan for World Government. It was not a system of theology which could be embraced by anyone without a change of status. A convert to it became a naturalised Jew, a member of the People of Israel, subject to the Mosaic Laws governing the nation.

This is what has constituted a problem for non-Jewish, and notably Christian understanding. Judaism has never been a faith that any individual could adhere to, simply by embracing its religious doctrine. Its accent was not on personal salvation, but on identification with a national mission to mankind. Of course, purity from idolatry was part of it, and Israel fully appreciated that the majority of mankind would never become Jews. But they could and would abandon idolatry and the evil ways that went with it. The Jews therefore welcomed Gentiles to their synagogues who had taken this step.

They were associates of Israel, "the stranger within the gates". What was required of them was the observance of what were called "The Laws of Noah", the precepts ultimately binding on the whole human race.

It was open to the individual, however, to go further. The Gentile could become a Jew by naturalization, a member of the people of Israel, identified with its mission to mankind, and obedient to its national code (the Law of Moses). Such a Gentile was regarded as having been reborn into his new identity: he was a "proselyte of righteousness", no longer a stranger and foreigner, but a fellow-citizen. He had become an Israelite, wholly and completely. The circumstances were almost totally different to those involving a personal change of religion.

But becoming an Israelite in the first century of the Christian Era was no light undertaking. The Land of Israel was under Roman government. At the head of that government in Rome was an emperor, who was also a god. Allegiance to the faith of Israel in complete seriousness could not fail to contemplate an apocalyptic climax in which the Roman Empire required to be overthrown: it was not simply a matter of morals. Therefore, for a Gentile to be a proselyte or even a God-fearer meant at this time making some response to the Messianic aspect, probably much more definite than for multitudes of born Jews. When, therefore, Jews arrived in due course in the synagogues of the Diaspora proclaiming the advent of Jesus as the Messianic king it was those who were not Jews by birth who were inevitably concerned and affected more ready to throw in their lot with the Messianists.

Christian teaching does not embrace these fundamental matters, though it is on record by the Roman historian Suetonius that the Emperor Claudius around the middle of the first century AD expelled the Jews from Rome because of Messianic Agitation. Among them, according to the Acts of the Apostles, were the followers of Jesus named Aquila with his wife Priscilla, both probably of Gentile origin.

The Jewish Messianists were ready to carry the war into the enemy's country by inserting passages into the prized *Sibylline Oracles*, such as the following:

"But when Rome shall rule over Egypt, though still delaying, then shall the great kingdom of the Immortal King appear among men, and a holy king shall come who shall have rule over the whole earth for all ages of the course of time. Then shall implacable wrath fall upon the men of Latium... Ah, wretched me, when shall that day come, and the judgement of Immortal God, the Great King?"

"And then the God of Heaven shall send a king and shall judge every man in blood and blazing fire. But there is a royal tribe whose seed shall not stumble, and it shall reign as time follows time, and shall begin to raise up the temple of God anew."

Fundamentally the Messianic was national and political in what it embraced. It had nothing to do with any divine saviour who sacrificed himself for human sin. Ample traces of the genuinely Messianic (original Christian) doctrine were preserved in the Gospels, composed in different parts of the Roman Empire in the last quarter of the first century AD.

It is as king of the Jews that Jesus is presented, especially in *Matthew* and *Luke*. The birth and infancy stories stress this status continually. As king, Jesus himself emphasised total loyalty to the Law of Moses (the national code) and proclaimed his immediate mission as confined to his own people. He instructs the Twelve, chosen to represent the Twelve Tribes of Israel, not to go to any Gentile, or even Samaritan centres.

In the Messianic Era they would sit on twelve thrones judging the tribes. Towards the end of his activities, directed wholly to recalling Israel to its world mission, he identified himself as Messiah by riding openly into Jerusalem as the king of Hebrew prophecy, thus throwing down the gauntlet to the alien Roman government.

The reader has to apprehend that anyone in any part of the Roman Empire who claimed to be a king without the authority of the Roman Emperor and Senate was committing high treason against Rome and would therefore be destroyed. In the case of Jesus he was condemned to the appropriate Roman torture, death by crucifixion. By notice fixed to the cross his crime was specified. What was the crime of Jesus? It had nothing to do with religion. Jesus had claimed to be "King of the Jews" without Roman licence. That was his crime.

Thus even when a Christian religion had begun to be created there remained on record testimony to the primitive nature and content of the Christian message as the fulfilment of Jewish national and political Messianism.

The transition was largely the outcome of the activities of Paul of Tarsus; though he himself had no design that this should be so. For him too the primary purpose of the Second Advent of Jesus was "to restore the kingdom to Israel" (*Acts* i. 6). And converted Gentiles would be part of Israel (*Eph.* ii. 11-14, 19). Is that *your* belief, Christian reader?

It was as the Christian outcome of the Jewish War with the Romans that the Gospels came into being. In the carnage of the War (67-70 AD) all the places associated with the activities of Jesus were in ruins and their inhabitants were substantially dead or taken captive, though some had fled. It was no longer practicable to obtain direct knowledge of the life and teaching of Jesus beyond what had got out of the country before the war. Consequently, when the Gospels were composed sixty to seventy years after the time of Jesus, not only did they reflect the ideas of the new religion of Christianity as this had developed in the Roman Empire in the meantime; they also contained a great deal of fiction to compensate for the paucity of genuine information available.

What was provided was in the nature of an historical novel, with its details varying and in contradiction, according to which part of the Roman Empire had seen its creation, and what were the resources and particular intentions of the creator.

What we have now to seek to recover with the benefit of historical and archaeological research is what is more reliable in the narratives, at the same time ascertaining to the extent practicable the methods and devices of each author in creating his version of the circumstances.

The points we have made here call for further exploration. The language of the Gospels is Greek, not Hebrew, though their theme is Jewish. This conveys that they were designed for a substantially Greek-speaking body of people who had come under the influence of the Christian propaganda, and now needed not only spiritual but biographical information about its Jewish hero. In written form this required to be made available, since communities of Christians had progressively come into existence around the Mediterranean and needed such material both for instruction and propaganda. The material, however, would not be uniform and identical, since it had not emanated from a central authority. Various individuals, some more reliably informed than others, had conveyed the details, and, as we shall have need to face, introduced their own embroidery and embellishments.

It is not known at what dates these compositions came to be described as Gospels. The word Gospel (Evangelion) was basically the "Good News" for the Jews that their awaited Messiah (Christ in Greek) and Deliverer had manifested himself. The version attributed to Luke tells of an angel who appeared to shepherds at Bethlehem, and informed them, "I bring you word of a great joy which will be shared by all the people, that to-day in David's town a deliverer has been born to you, none other than the Lord Messiah."

As I have indicated, the demand for Gospels increased at the very time that reliable information had become almost impossible to obtain because of the destruction wrought in Israel by the Roman armies. And inevitably many of them, in the fashion of Greek composition relating to ancient heroes, with which we can compare them, were becoming adorned with miracle and legend.

The Gospels included in the New Testament are fairly responsible in their composition, and they could have been included for this reason. But they may also have been chosen as representative of particular geographical areas in the Roman Empire.

But behind all Christian Gospels was other material conveying the Good News of the Messiah's advent. Traditionally we learn of two little books which evangelists took with them. One was a collection of proof-texts from the Old Testament held to relate to the Messiah with indications of how they had been fulfilled in the activities of Jesus. The other was a small collection of sayings and teachings ascribed to him.

It was probably, as much as anything, the failure of the Second Advent to materialise and the deaths of the immediate Apostles of Jesus, that stimulated a demand for further information. But as I have pointed out the sources of information were virtually dried up as a consequence of the Jewish War with the Romans, and Gospel writers in the latter part of the first century had to call upon their imagination to amplify their resources.

Of the canonical Gospels the only one with a respectable apostolic derivation is *Mark*, according to traditional information. It reflects the recollections of the Galilean fisherman Simon called Peter. Simon's native tongue was Galilean Aramaic, and consequently in his travels in the West to speak about his association with Jesus he required an interpreter. His need was met by a young man, John Mark.

Mark, according to Papias of Hierapolis, when acting as Peter's interpreter, "wrote down accurately everything he remembered, though not strictly in order, of what had been said and done by Christ." After Peter's martyrdom these notes taken by Mark were worked up into a book, probably composed in Italy around 75-80 AD. Chapter xiii of *Mark's* Gospel in the New Testament indicates a lapse of time. As we would expect the document contains no Nativity material, and is presented in short sections. The end of the book is missing. It breaks off suddenly where the women of Jesus's company find the tomb open and a young man there tells them that Jesus has risen. In the New Testament a substitute ending has been provided.

Mark's Gospel, inevitably, was of positive service to later writers like *Matthew* and *Luke*, which is why the three Gospels are known as the *Synoptics* (Common Viewpoint Gospels). It provided a biographical outline of the activities of Jesus, resting, reliably as it seemed, on the testimony of a close associate. Into such a framework other elements, of a bogus or doubtful character, could readily be introduced to amplify the material and give it a slant in accordance with each Evangelist's aims and concerns.

While *Mark* is subsequent to the Fall of Jerusalem in AD 70, *Matthew* and *Luke* will therefore be later still. Both Gospels give evidence of the lapse of time. At the end of Matthew, when the body of Jesus was found missing from the tomb, the guards posted there were instructed to say, "His disciples came by night and stole him while we slept."

The author finishes by saying, "And this is the version that is current among the Jews to this day." With *Luke* the indication of the passage of time comes at the very beginning of the Gospel, where the author states that prior to himself many others had "endeavoured to draw up an account of those matters held by us to be fact, exactly as they transmitted them to us who initially were the eyewitnesses and bearers of the Message." At this stage we do not need to enter into the particular aims of each Evangelist.

With *John's* Gospel we have an altogether different set of circumstances, which lie outside the Petrine tradition. We will be considering these in due course. But with this Gospel also we have evidence of late date. At its close the resurrected Jesus appears to his followers by the Sea of Galilee. Peter is informed that he will die a martyr's death. Following behind them is the Beloved Disciple of Jesus. Jealously Peter asks Jesus, "What about him, Master?" Jesus replies, "Supposing I wish him to remain until I come, what concern is that of yours? You follow me." The comment then follows: "Thus the saying got about among the brothers that that disciple would not die, though Jesus never told him he would not die, he only said, "Supposing I wish him to remain until I come, what concern is that of yours?" He is the disciple who testified to these matters and recorded them, and we know that his testimony is trustworthy."

According to tradition John the Beloved Disciple was still alive early in the second century AD, when at the request of the Christians in Asia Minor he dictated his recollections of Jesus. These formed the groundwork of the Fourth Gospel.

Thus in the case of three out of the four Gospels in the New Testament we have evidence that they were late compositions, remote by from 60 to 70 years from the circumstances to which they relate.

The choice of the four Gospels did not rest on their verifiable authenticity, leaving aside the matter of their divine inspiration. They reflected the spread of the Christian Faith throughout the Roman Empire, and the pressing need for an agreed expression of it which would

overcome the inevitable tendency to sectarianism resulting from the different ideas of missionaries combined
with local pagan religious backgrounds in different countries. There had rapidly been self-evident a variety of beliefs and doctrines which before long would have
brought about the almost total disintegration of the
Christian body. One means of coping with the situation
was to make choice of four acceptable versions of the
Gospel story as authoritative, roughly representative of
the north, south, east and west of the Mediterranean
area.

The next stage was the creation of a body of Christian
Scriptures, styled the New Testament, of equal authority
with the Jewish Scriptures, now to be termed the Old
Testament. In this development, made practicable by the
adhesion of the Roman Empire to the Christian Faith
under Constantine, the four Gospels would become dig-
nified as a part of the Word of God, divinely inspired,
and their presumed authors would be presented as
Saints. The contradictions between the contents of the
several Gospels were not deemed to present any difficulty.

But the Gospels were actually written individually, and
with no thought of a New Testament in view, to meet the
needs of Christian communities in different areas. They
were in a sense a substitute for the failure of a Second
Advent to materialise. While presenting an outline of the
activities of Jesus leading up to his atoning death and resurrection, they increasingly amplified his moral and
ethical teachings, since these would be what was of most
service communally and in a social environment. This
was especially necessary in relation to political authorities, with whom the Christians were in bad odour as
rebels and lawless and anti-social activists.

It is not easy for Christians to appreciate that Christianity did not begin as a new religion in which Jesus
played a part as a divine incarnation. The mission of Jesus himself as the ultimate king (the Messiah—anointed

one) his people were awaiting was exclusively to the Jewish nation. This fact is still preserved in *Matthew's* Gospel, where Jesus instructs the Twelve, "Keep away from Gentile centres, and do not enter any Samaritan town. Go instead to the lost sheep of the house of Israel" (ch. x). Also in Matthew's version of the encounter of Jesus with the Syro-Phoenician woman, who sought help for her sick daughter, Jesus declares (xiv. 24), "I have only been sent to the lost sheep of the house of Israel."

The beginnings of a change arose out of the proclamation of Jesus to Gentiles as developed by Paul. Though even he would have it that all non-Jews who gave their allegiance to Jesus had thereby become Israelites. As Paul wrote to the Ephesians: "So bear in mind that you were once Gentiles in the physical sense, who are termed the Uncircumcision by those termed in respect of an operation in the flesh the Circumcision, because at that time you were without benefit of Christ, aliens to the body politic of Israel, and strangers to the covenants of promise. But now in Christ Jesus you who were once far off have been brought near by the blood of Christ... So now you are no longer strangers and foreigners, but fellow-citizens of the saints" (*Eph.* ii. 10-19).

But after Paul's death, and especially after the destruction of Jerusalem and the Temple in 70 AD, there was nothing to attach converted Gentiles to the Jewish people. The Messianic element of the Jewish heritage was taken over and absorbed into a paganised faith constituting a new religion. The canonical Gospels reflect the transition progressively; and of course later the breakaway of Christianity from Judaism would be intensified and have its effect on Gospel manuscripts.

It is the function of the historian to seek to get behind the scenes and relate the authority of the Gospels to what can be gleaned of the transition process, particularly in the theological context. A committed Christian cannot be expected to achieve this. Hence the dilemma of many modern Churchmen, especially as the pagan aspect of

Christianity is so beguiling. The future will show what will be the outcome—perhaps a rebirth of the Messianic to change for the better the course of history.

The quotations from the New Testament in this book are from Dr. Schonfield 's edition and translation of the New Testament THE ORIGINAL NEW TESTAMENT. This is the only one in the English language reflecting the style of each writer and the structure of the individual books.

Messianic for Modern Man

Christianity has its roots in Messianic Judaism. It owes its name and its very being to the belief that Jesus was the Messiah (the Christ) whom the people of Israel were eagerly expecting two thousand years ago. The original gospel was the Good News that the Messiah had appeared. He had been killed by the rulers of this world, but had been raised from the dead, ascended into the presence of God, and would shortly return to inaugurate the reign of God throughout the earth after executing judgement on the evil and idolatrous who opposed themselves to the principles of the theocracy. The agents of God and associates of the Messiah in establishing the New Order would be the foreordained people of God, Israel, and membership of this people was now open in advance of the Messiah's return to individuals of all nations who turned to the worship of the One God, received pardon by an act of Divine grace in virtue of the atoning work of the Messiah which he had performed at his first appearance by offering himself as a living sacrifice. The reward for present adherence to the terms of the New Order would be participation in its felicities.

Stripped of all accretions and corruptions this is the essence of Christianity. It did not begin as a new religion, but as the embryo of a system of righteous world government designed and revealed by God as the perfect way of life for mankind. Preparation for this ultimate development had been proceeding progressively since the creation of man in the choice first of a family and then of a nation as the witnesses of God, and tbe recipients of his commandments and revelations of the future. Within the nation, for purposes of the plan, there was chosen a priestly order and a royal house, from which would issue ideal ministers and an ideal ruler. The stage of the coming of the ruler had been reached with the raising up of Jesus of the line of David, and the succeeding stage of calling out and completing the redeemed and redeeming people is now in train.

The character of Christianity is inescapably Messianic, deriving its claims and objectives from the Jewish Bible and Jewish teaching, seeing itself as the culmination of a process spiritually traced out In the history of the Hebrews set down in the Old Testament. The fulfilment of the Divine Plan of the Ages is the primary concern. Emphasis is on the individual chiefly as a member of the chosen Community, contributing by his conduct to the advancement of the common purpose or to retarding it. It is not his ego as a distinct person which receives consideration, though as one of the company of the Elect he can obtain Divine help and guidance.

Christianity has now to get past its semi-pagan phase which has persisted through so many centuries. To accomplish this the inclination must be resisted to devote too much attention to metaphysics. Instead, effort should be directed to recapturing and restating the Church's original messianism, since this constituted the purpose of its creation and alone justifies its existence. It was foreseen from the beginning that when the times of the Gentiles should be fulfilled Church and Synagogue would be reunited. With this reunion a further unfoldment of the Divine purpose for mankind would take place. Without it neither Christianity nor Judaism have any place in the scheme of things, and help for humanity in the perilous path of its evolution must come from another quarter.

The conditions are propitious for Christianity to set about casting away its idols and returning to full purity of faith in the Unity of God. When this is done Judaism will be able to advance to the acceptance of Jesus as the Messiah who came at the appointed time.

The common watchword will be "One God and one Messiah" (EIS THEOS KAI CHRISTOS). The road will be open for the kingdoms and states of this world to become those of our Lord and of His Christ.

The task of the Messianic Movement, as I may call it, which will supersede Judaism and Christianity, will not be to make a new religion, but to make a new world. Mankind no longer needs religions. The movement will identify itself as a spiritually-conscious community which anyone who accepts its principles may join. This character, it may be said, was foreshadowed in the Old and New Testament doctrine of a chosen people, a priestly or ministering nation. It will be the vehicle of the promotion of world unity, welfare and peace, thus fulfilling the promise of a Messianic Age.

I have been rehearsing here in brief the convictions to which I have been led by study, meditation and discussions with many people, ever since in my youth I accepted Jesus as the Messiah. It has been a great privilege, though it has not lacked its sorrows, to know Christianity and Judaism equally well and to be compelled to seek out what was of enduring worth in both. Progressively I have found myself having to convert the rigid into the fluid in order to obtain motion towards the future which could carry forward vital intimations from the oast into an area of wider application and consequence. I have had a sense of guidance in these things, and I must not shrink from using the term, ever since I was a child. There have been moments of acute vision, which I have disclosed to few, and do not wish to publicise, which have involved taking unexpected and far-reaching action. Since the results are visible it will suffice if in this book I simply speak my mind to the best of my ability on matters which concern us all.

It is not inappropriate, since Jesus was a Jew, that a Jew who acknowledges him to have been the Messiah should intervene in an endeavour to assist Christians in resolving the spiritual problems many of them are facing to-day. I have great sympathy with their difficulties, and perhaps from my background, as well as from a lifetime of study for my own enlightenment, I am more conscious of certain of the causes than they are themselves.

Very early in my own spiritual pilgrimage I was confronted with the realisation that the Gentile mind approached the Being of God differently. There was an innate disposition to want to bring God into closer affinity with man, which it had taken the Jews in their former pagan state as revealed in the Old Testament a great while to overcome. Christianity, founded upon the Jewish doctrine of a Messiah, produced a faith, due largely to Pauline Christology, which while it provided a partial emancipation from paganism also satisfied the Gentile need for contact with a human element in deity. Modern thought having challenged mythology, traditional Christianity became open to serious questioning as to how much of it was still valid, especially its theological structure.

There was another difference to be seen in the Gentile attitude of mind. This came from an Indo-European heritage in which self- consciousness played a prominent part, and which accordingly stressed the continuing entity of the individual. When Christianity was born the mystery cults had been responding to the longing for personal salvation. Christian doctrine made such salvation available much more freely on simple terms of faith, blending the individual eternal hope with the more corporate Messianic hope. But here again, without a Heaven and a Hell, what did salvation signify to-day?

I found in Christianity a too great aptness to systematize theologically, a further Gentile trait, as if it were possible to treat religion as a science and use the Bible as an infallible text book.

The discovery is now in process of being made that not only is Christianity unscientific, but that perhaps in essence it is not even a religion. This is a shock to the orthodox way of thinking, even if it should prove to be a salutary one. I would suggest, however, that it is not profitable to quest for a fresh formula or modes of expression in order to preserve In some fashion ideas which ought to be discarded. The aim should be to release Christianity from bondage to the belief that it is a final revelation, so that the suppressed Hebraic life in it can germinate afresh in the universal context which first started Christianity on its way.

The service of my life has been devoted to two major activities which are closely related. Through one of them I have delved into the past, and through the other I have projected myself into the future. Both activities have been concerned with a philosophy of life, the detection of a progressive purpose in the story of mankind, which illuminated the way ahead and inspired the particular contribution I have made to the promotion of a united world.

It is no credit to me that I have engaged in these pursuits, since as I must disclose, though the telling is with great reluctance, I have been impelled to do so by promptings I could not disobey. Some who know me have been puzzled, and even irked, by my confidence and assurance in many things I have said and done, especially as what I advocated was frequently in conflict with prevailing opinion and sometimes contrary to my own natural attitude of mind. Very rarely, and never completely, could I bring myself to say what was at the back of my convictions, preferring to seek for convincing arguments in favour of what I contended. If reasoning did not succeed it would be unlikely that a revelation of my experiences would do so. This would certainly be true of the majority, and it would have been of no help in my work to be thought of as peculiar and visionary. I should have gathered around me almost inevitably some who would be chiefly interested in the experiences, which they would relate to their own spiritual systems and concepts, and there would be included those who would claim me as one of high spiritual degree.

While I feel that I ought no longer to be silent about what has so largely been responsible for my outlook and activities, since it explains how my life and thinking has been shaped, I have to make clear my belief that I have been used, as many others have been and will be, because it was necessary, and not because I am of any special consequence. Those who do not know me may be assured that I have a full measure of defects, and I beg them to lay no stress whatever on what would be completely false, an assumption that I have in any way merited my employment. Of what good things may be said of me, one, I suppose, is that I have resolutely refused to allow myself to be regarded as a Master or Teacher, to found a cult or benefit materially by such service as I have given to mankind. This to me would so utterly have dishonoured what inspiration I have had that I would be guilty of treating it as a lie. When I am saying this I do not want it to be inferred that any words of mine have a higher than human wisdom. My ideas are the outcome of my own studies and meditations. But the direction they have taken appears to me to have a certain rightness which has not depended on my skill and scholarship, and which occasionally has been quite unexpected and surprising. Only at rare moments have I had a startling clarity of perception.

Judaism and Christianity are the primary Messianic faiths. They conceive of man as placed in this world by God to accomplish a purpose the outcome of which will be an ideal state of human society having knowledge of God and obeying his laws. The purpose is to be fulfilled by means of a definite plan progressively revealed to those entrusted with its furtherance, in order to secure their active co-operation. The plan clarifies the methods to be employed and involves successive stages of development. The whole process is related to human history, and gives a meaning to history: its time- chart covers thousands of years, and allows for setbacks and changes of emphasis arising from human failings, resistance and inertia. According to this concept every contingency has been foreseen from the beginning; but the plan, since it is God's, cannot fail, and his will assures that ultimately it will come to fruition.

With Messianism there is nothing fortuitous in the experiences of man. Whether he is aware of it or not he is evolving under guidance and his destiny is in no doubt. He has the power to assert himself, to revolt, and temporarily to his own discomfort and suffering to get out of line but nothing he may at any time do can permanently affect the success of the plan. Equally to his own happiness and well-being man can learn more about the plan and consciously cooperate in its promotion.

Messianism is thus the expression of a theocratic programme for world government, though the theocracy it envisages is not a Divine dictatorship, but democracy taking its initiatives from communion with the wisdom of God. It asserts that man has a nature which links him with God, and that he has a built-in desire for the things which God wants Man is brought into relationship with God as to the centre of his own being and of all being, and is connected with God by a spiritual umbilical cord as a channel of communication.

Easter 1966

For nineteen centuries the Church has centred its faith on the worth to the individual of the Crucifixion and Resurrection of Jesus Christ. By penitent acceptance of the infallible virtue of the Crucifixion as an act of atonement for human sin the individual would escape the just punishment of sin in the Hereafter, and participate in the blissful immortality assured and guaranteed by the Resurrection.

It was the Apostle Paul who first set out this doctrine, and its influence from the beginning and down the centuries has been profound. Not only did it help to overcome the fear of death and of the mysterious Beyond: it lent to the experience of life itself a capacity to overcome evil and to endure present ills with cheerfulness and fortitude. The doctrine may thus be said to have fully justified itself and to have produced in countless instances highly beneficial results. It has had great psychological value.

Even today with our deeper understanding of the human ego and of causes and effects we can see the efficacy of a creed so positive in the dogmatic simplicity of its propositions. Increasing 'knowledge of the universe and of the processes of evolution has rocked theology and made God far more difficult to comprehend than when He wore His older image: but it has not driven out the significance for the individual with faith of a Divine act of Incarnation.

Yet it can and is now being questioned whether the real intention of Christianity is what the Church made of it under instruction by St. Paul. Was he in fact correct in his Christology? Did Jesus ever conceive himself to be Divine in the manner afterwards depicted in particular in the Gospel of St. John?

Historical inquiry casts the gravest doubts on the Church's early interpretations and compels us to reexamine the beliefs and teaching of Jesus himself, so far as research makes them available to us.

We discover that for him the emphasis of what he held to be his mission was Messianic, the inauguration of the transformation of human society, the bringing to birth of a redeemed world enlisted in the service of God by the adjustment of the relationships between man and God and between man and his fellows. Jesus saw his own suffering as the means, prophetically anticipated, for promoting the Great Change, suffering which would be shared by his followers as the nucleus of the redeeming community. His faithfulness, and theirs, would win victory over death itself, giving assurance of the coming time when death would increasingly be conquered and finally abolished among men. Medical science is now forecasting much the same thing in its own way.

But history equally apprises us of how this vision became affected by Hellenic individualism and the pagan Saviour cults, so that emerging Christianity—especially when the expected return of Christ did not materialise—was turned more and more towards a personal salvation and a hope that lay elsewhere than in a world of the senses. All that was physical was evil, and man must seek release into total absorption in God or into a state of existence akin to that of angels in the home of God which was Heaven. Christianity became committed to the unearthly, its contentions inevitably appearing less and less valid the nearer man approached to the Age of Reason and greater maturity of mind.

Desperately Christian theology has been seeking to salvage what it can of the content of its former positions by erudite argument. It cannot yet perceive that its dilemma arises from an ancient submission to teaching never originated by Christ himself. After so many centuries of authoritative teaching, given out as it is claimed under the guidance of the Holy Spirit, it is hard to admit that the way of the Church has not been that of Jesus, and that he was far more in the right of it in seeing that the task of the Messianic Community was the creation of the Good Society for mankind. Many Christians do see this nowadays, and these are more directly carrying out the mandate of their Master.

We do not have to abandon the historical Christ with Mr. Allegro or think in terms of a religionless Christianity with the Bishop of Woolwich. But we do have to come to the point of confessing that for man the nature of God is impossible to discover, to depict, or to demonstrate, and to agree that the Church was not divinely entrusted with any function to attempt this impossibility. God Is to be known by man only within the area of man's legitimate concerns, the conversion of his planet into a paradise. All visions and apprehensions of God as our common Father are to be understood as designed to this end. In the words of the Bible, "Heaven, even the heavens are the Lord's, but the earth hath He given to the children of men."

The Church went off the rails as soon as it began to impress itself on heathenism by devising a theology culminating in stating its findings in a creed.

The true and effective incarnation lies in the grace bestowed on man in having the potential to become more noble, more worthy, more responsive to the betterment of his kind. The goal of Adam is still to achieve Sonship of God, to reflect in his proper realm the likeness of God. So much of the venerable myth has present relevance. The road ahead will doubtless involve many crucifixions, many resurrections. In this respect it will be long before the pioneer example and leadership of Jesus ceases to inspire and spur us on.

God or Mammon?

From Gold Standard to a God Standard

Because we are proclaiming a way of salvation for Mankind it is inevitable that the international lawyers and the scribes of the economists should come to us with their cunning and challenging questions.

They want to know where we stand, whether we are orthodox or unorthodox, what economic system we advocate and what policy of monetary reform we favour. "Do we not agree," they urge, "that the Economic Problem is the weightiest of all the problems affecting world order?" Some of us, momentarily forgetting the freedom of the sons of God, are prone to answer simply "Yes." Others fear to give offence to the experts, or seek to escape with a plea of ignorance of technical matters.

Yet fundamentally the real ignorance is on the side of our questioners, and we must dare to be no less searching in our answers. After all, Economics is primarily a mechanism for convenience of trade between foreigners. When trade began to travel men needed currency for their commerce. Barter meant the carrying of heavy bales, only profitable in dishonest dealing with backward peoples. In civilised lands coinage was substituted, and finally because even this was unwieldy when negotiations grew to a scale of millions transactions were by credits with a backing represented by an accepted wealth-standard. The leading standard hitherto has been gold, because it was precious, portable and imperishable, as well as negotiable.

This standard suffices no longer for world trade because it is lacking in one essential quality; it is not universal. That is to say, some countries produce it and

others do not. It is also virtually useless except for orna-
ment and a few scientific purposes. It is therefore both
wasteful and futile to buy and store it in vaults if you
have not got it. Neither the precious nor portable qualities of gold are any longer valid. Nowadays the alternative
wealth-standard of productive capacity (manufacturing
power—the combination of the work of man and machine) is being substituted; but this is quite literally an
artificial standard. It must fail in the universal sense because of inequality of supplies, labour and living conditions.

Essentially, therefore, the quest for a universal economic standard is akin to the quest for an impartial
world authority, and the problem of a medium of exchange is similar to the problem of international medi-
ation. The conception of an international bank is linked
with the conception of a federal commonwealth of nations. We are all the time seeking for an expression of the
universal and the absolute.

What is this expression but a reflection of God, who is
the One Good, Absolute, Universal and Eternal? We have
to change from a Gold Standard to a God Standard,
which is what Jesus meant when he spoke of the impossibility of serving both God and Mammon, and that
we should lay up our treasure in Heaven (that is, in
God).

We have said above that "all Economics is primarily a
mechanism for convenience of trade between foreigners." Only in God, the Father of All, do we cease to be
foreigners. We are no more "strangers and aliens, but
fellow-citizens of the holy (nation), and relatives of God"
(Eph. ii. 19). On earth the Holy Nation is the embodi-
ment of the true standard, the Sovereignty of God and
the Brotherhood of Man made manifest. It follows, then,
that we here of this communion represent in ourselves
the world standard, the new sterling.

We glimpse this truth in a famous, but badly translated passage in St. Paul's Second Letter to the Corinthi-

ans, which we should accurately render: "Therefore he that is in Christ is a new product: the old status has gone; essentially it has become new. And all things are of God, who through the agency of Christ has exchanged our currency for His own, and has given us the administration of the changed coinage. So that it was in fact God changing in Christ the world currency for His own, not calculating its debasement against it, and has placed on deposit with us the sum realised by the exchange. We are accordingly negotiators of Christ, as though God by us was making the proposition; we give the invitation on Christ's behalf, 'Be changed to the Divine standard'" (II Cor. V. 17-20).

So then we are a living and abiding credit, backed by the inextinguishable wealth of the Divine resources. In the coming time the whole world's currency will be pegged to us, and our authority in all lands will be sufficient cover for every transaction. We shall release wealth from bondage, and all will have abundance.

Should 'Things Strangled' be Omitted from Acts xv. 29?

In the course of some recent studies in the Sermon on the Mount I made a discovery, though perhaps this is rather too strong a term, which happens to throw light on the vexed question of the text of the Apostolic decree in Acts 15. The new evidence which I am able to bring forward seems to show that the Western Text is right in omitting 'things strangled' from the number of prohibitions. The late Professor Peake discussed the problem in a recent article.[8]

'The question as to the decree and the four prohibitions,' he wrote, 'is one of the most tangled problems in the history of the early Church. There is, in the first place, a serious variation of text. According to the generally accepted text we have apparently three food prohibitions combined with one ethical. But there are very early and important witnesses which omit the reference to "things strangled." If this text is correct, it is still possible to suppose that, apart from the ethical, we have two food prohibitions. But the removal of "things strangled" makes it possible to take all three as ethical, that is, as prohibitions of idolatry, murder, and impurity.'[9]

It is well known that the evidence of the earliest MSS is against the omission, while the external evidence is in favour. If 'things strangled' is retained, it is very difficult to regard the decree as historical. As Canon Wilson says: 'There is the incongruity, which must have struck every one, of coupling with these food-laws the prohibition of fornication, as if it were on a level with them. There is

8 'Paul and the Jewish Christians,' *Bulletin of The John Rylands Library*, Jan. 1929, pp. 31-62.
9 P. 45.

the unaccountable omission of all mention of circumcision, which from 15.5 we see was the thing chiefly insisted on. There is the inconsistency of saying in the decree that "they would not trouble them which from among the Gentiles turn to God," and then imposing on them food-laws which there is evidence to show were not generally observed among the Jews of the Dispersion, as seems also to have been admitted by St. Peter (15.10). There is the statement, in the Bezan text, of Ac 21.25, "we sent, giving judgment that they should observe nothing of that sort. There is the strange statement (in 15.31) that, when the decree was reported at Antioch, "the multitude rejoiced for the consolation." There is the still more inexplicable fact that St. Paul, shortly afterwards, when the question about the eating of meat "sold in the shambles" (1 Co 10.25) which had been offered to idols, does not allude to this decree, while he absolutely forbids (1 Co 10.20-21) sharing in idol feasts. And, finally, there is the fact that no Western Father, or apologist, or hostile critic, ever alludes to such a food-law as enjoined on Christians. If it ever existed it was ignored from the first.'[10]

In his next paragraph the same writer concludes that 'if the words "things strangled" were not in the decree, the natural interpretation of the decree would, beyond all question, have been that it forbade the three great sins of idolatry, murder,,and fornication; and was, in fact, a purely moral law.'[11]

Professor Peake found it 'extraordinary that the Gentile disciples should be told that nothing more would be required from them than to abstain from idolatry, murder, and fornication. The reference to murder in par-

10 The Acts of the Apostles, translated from the Codex Bezae, Introduction, pp. 16-17.
11 Ibid. Canon Wilson notes the association in Rev 2215, ' Without are the fornicators, and the murderers, and the idolaters. '

ticular,' he felt, 'is difficult to accept. It is hardly credible that it should be necessary to prohibit this in Christian Churches.'[12] He therefore decided 'that the text with four prohibitions is correct, three of these having definitely to do with forbidden forms of food.'[13]

Will not the difficulty be overcome, if it can be proved that it was just these three ethical commandments that were regarded by the Pharisees and by the Lord Jesus Himself as fundamental for society? So we have it already in the Mishnah:

'Captivity enters the world on account of idol-worship, fornication, and bloodshed.'[14]

Elsewhere, it is said, 'Whoso slandereth his neighbour committeth sins as great as idolatry, fornication, and murder.'[15] And, indeed, so fundamental were these three commandments regarded by the Rabbis in the stress of the times that they declare, 'Any sin denounced by the Law may be committed by a man if his life is threatened, except the sins of idolatry, fornication, and murder.'[16]

To the Jewish religious authorities, then, the commandments concerning idolatry, fornication, and murder were τούτων τῶν ἐπάναγκες 'these compulsory things,' exactly what the Jewish Christian elders and apostles call them in the decree (15.28).

The Sermon on the Mount is evidence that this view was held by the Pharisees at an earlier date, for Jesus, in setting forth the righteousness of the Law which should exceed that of the Pharisees, comments first on these very same commandments; murder (Mt 5.21), fornication (Mt 5.27), and idolatry (Mt 5.33). It may be objected that the last deals not with idolatry but oaths. But this is answered by understanding that Jesus condemned

12 P. 47.
13 P. 48.
14 Aboth, v. 9.
15 Ercch. fol. xv. B.
16 Sanhed. fol. lxxiv. A.

swearing on the ground that it indirectly countenanced idolatry. The heathen might suppose, if Jews swore by any created thing, that they too were polytheists. And if Jews accustomed themselves to such oaths they might be led to use the oaths of the heathen as well, and so God's name would be profaned. Hence the Rabbis forbade partnership with a heathen, 'lest at any time the heathen should impose an oath on the Jew, and he be obliged to swear by the heathen's idol; and the Law says (Ex 23.13), "Make no mention of the name of other gods, neither let it be heard out of thy mouth."'[17]

We may infer, I think, that Jesus knew of the Pharisee teaching on the fundamental character of these commandments.

Professor Peake admitted that ethical prohibitions would harmonize better with all the circumstances than food-laws, but he was too honest a scholar to adopt this interpretation without a valid reason and merely to evade a difficulty. Perhaps the additional evidence which I have adduced may be found adequate to show that after all there is justification for omitting 'things strangled,' and that on this issue, at any rate, the Western text is to be preferred.

Article in the Expository Times December 1929

17 Sanhed. fol. lxiii. B.

Fraud and Forgery in Early Christianity

It is most unlikely that a true account of early Christianity will ever be forthcoming at all comprehensively, even if we should fortunately come into possession of many more sources of information than we have at present. The historical circumstances are all against it. Too many documents were destroyed and too much was never recorded. Yet thanks to research and chance discoveries we are now in a position to know much more of what really happened than was possible formerly.

Progress was extremely difficult while religious enquiry was inhibited by religious bigotry, and while the Bible was treated as an inerrant authority. Even today, many orthodox Christians—including learned theologians—cling to the notion that their Faith came into being as a result of spiritual revelation, and, therefore, is not affected by the processes applicable to the investigation of secular matters. Some clergy contrive to their own satisfaction to occupy contradictory positions, like the gentleman who in Biblical scholarship was Professor Brown but on issues of faith was Canon Brown.

It would be asking too much of the believer to expect him to be wholly objective in his approach to the origins of his creed. But we do have to insist that in historical and literary research the same standards of judgment have to be employed for religious questions as for all others. It is only fair to say that the best Christian scholars accept this, and their studies have been of the greatest possible assistance. The New Testament itself makes evident to anyone who reads it without prior assumptions that it furnishes ample evidence of manipulation and corruption. Christianity as we know it emerged as the outcome of practice and activities which, in the light of more advanced ethical conduct we

would regard as highly reprehensible. When the early
Christians and their leaders are described as saints this
does not at all imply what we would think of as the attributes of saintliness.

The aspect of early Christianity which we are to consider is crucial and has far-reaching consequences. It
affects not only literary and historical issues, but our
whole approach to the formation of convictions. By no
means does it destroy faith in spiritual values and superhuman agencies and processes. But it does demonstrate the artificiality of much that we may have
supposed to be incontrovertible truth.

At the present day, in Communism, we have an eloquent example of how it can be deemed perfectly legitimate in the interests of an ideology to employ forgery
and fraud, to erase and alter inconvenient records, to
concoct false statements and misrepresent the views of
opponents. The very same things were a commonplace
in ancient times, and had an even better chance of es-
caping detection.

I am sure that you are fully familiar with what went
on in the Classical period, when there were no laws of
copyright and indications of quotation were frequently
omitted. Writers constantly borrowed from the works of
other authors and passed off the passages as their own.
Historians composed speeches for their historical per-
sonages to deliver expressing sentiments which were
considered appropriate to the occasion and to the person concerned, but which were therefore largely or entirely fictitious. The interests of propaganda prompted
worse abuses, and also the desire for gain. Books were
forged in the name of the famous, whose genuine writings had to be distinguished by scholars from the fakes.
To get his own ideas into circulation a propagandist
would think nothing of introducing them by interpolation the works of some well-known authority, or changing that author's language so that he was made to
express himself in a different sense. Where so many

people were illiterate or uncritical they could all the more readily be deceived.

The Jews in the Hellenic world behaved no differently. Anxious to convert the heathen from idolatry they interpolated suitable Greek literature. To quote the Rev. Bate, "Orpheus was made to recant his polytheism and proclaim the one true God; Sophocles to foretell the end of the world by fire and the future blessedness of the righteous. All this was merely a forcible entry upon the heritage of the Hellenes; the major premiss underlying it was the genuine conviction that the order of revelation was in fact older and truer than the wisdom and worship of the Greek."

Notably, to attack Rome, Jews added numerous predictions to the famous Sibylline Oracles, and they were followed later by the Christians. When Caesar Augustus became Pontifex Maximus he had a quantity of spurious oracles burnt, and his successor Tiberius also instituted a purification of the collection because of a popular prophecy that the end of the Empire was at hand. Here is an extract from one of the forged oracles.

"But when Rome shall rule over Egypt, though still delaying, then shall the great kingdom of the immortal King appear among men, and a holy king shall come (i.e. the Messiah) who shall rule over the whole earth for all ages of the course of time. Then shall implacable wrath fall upon the men of Latium... Ah, wretched me, when shall that day come, and the judgment of immortal God, the great King? Yet still be ye builded, ye cities, and all adorned with temples and theatres, with market squares and images of gold, silver and stone, that so ye may come to the day of bitterness. For it shall come, when the smell of brimstone shall pass upon all men."

But even among the later books of the Old Testament and in the Apocrypha there are forged prophecies and writings attributed falsely to ancient worthies. Especially when the succession of Jewish prophets had ceased, sects like the Essenes, in order to spread their teaching, composed books in the names of the former prophets and patriarchs. These are commonly classified as Pseudepigrapha. The learned were probably not deceived, but ignorant people would regard them as genuine and inspired. One of the most esteemed of these works was the Book of Enoch. Enoch was one of the antediluvian patriarchs mentioned in Genesis, who was believed to have been taken alive to heaven. The forged book was accepted as genuine by the early Christians and a saying from it is quoted in the Epistle of Jude as the actual words of Enoch. Incidentally, the Epistle of Jude, supposedly a brother of James and therefore of Jesus, is almost certainly a forgery.

This brings us to the New Testament, where the practice of forging and tampering with documents is Specifically attested. In the Second Epistle of Paul to the Thessalonians we find the author saying, "Now I beg you, brothers, as regards the coming of our Lord Jesus Christ and our being gathered to him, not to take speedy leave of your senses or become agitated, either by a spirit intimation, or by a speech, or by any letter purporting to be from me, under the impression that the Day of the Lord has began."

And at the end he writes, "The greeting I subjoin in my own, Paul's, hand. It is the mark of authenticity on every letter. This is how I write." Then follows the greeting, "The lovingkindness of the Lord Jesus Christ be with you all." It is clearly conveyed that forged letters of Paul were in circulation.

Elsewhere, at the close of the Book of Revelation, we read, "I testify to all who hear the prophetic words of this book, that if anyone shall add to them God will add to him the plagues set down in this book. And if anyone subtracts from the words of the book of this prophecy God will subtract from him his share in the Tree of Life, and in the Holy City, the matters recorded in this book." The author obviously felt the need to safeguard his work by putting a curse on anyone who thought to interfere? with the text.

But before we look more closely at the New Testament itself let us look at early Christian literature in general.

For the second and third centuries A.D. we have access to a considerable number of Christian writings, and therefore to a substantial amount of evidence. In this period there was no uniformity of Christian belief. There was much rivalry between churches and a variety of expressions of doctrine. As a result the practice of fraud and forgery flourished, and was made easier by the fact that the majority of Christians were illiterate and ignorant and extremely gullible, and by the lack of knowledge of what had actually been written by the first century apostles and evangelists.

Particularly because of the Jewish wars with the Romans, especially that of A.D.66-70, the churches in other lands had been cut off from the parent authority in Jerusalem, and it was not known how much of its teaching and literature had survived. To this day no first century Christian documents in Hebrew and Aramaic have been recovered. Neither could it be known, because no catalogue existed, what was the extent and character of the writings attributable to those who had seen and known Jesus, In these circumstances the door was wide open, either in the interest of advocating various teachings or to lend prestige to different Christian communities, for the composition of writings purporting to be the work of apostolic and other notabilities.

In 1924 a former Provost of Eton, the late Dr. Montague Rhodes James, prepared and translated a collection of such compositions under the title *The Apocryphal New Testament*. The volume consists almost entirely of Gospels, Acts, Epistles and Apocalypses with false ascriptions and in substance fictitious. Some of the documents can be described as pious romances which would deceive very few; but others are wilfully fraudulent. Taken as a whole they attest that it was common among the early Christians to employ forgery as an instrument of propaganda.

In certain instances the intention was to answer awkward questions which were being asked. For example: if Jesus was Divine how could he suffer and die? and why did he perform no miracles before he was thirty years of age?

So Gospels were written, like the Gospel of Peter, which declared that when Jesus was on the cross he experienced no pain, and various so-called *Infancy Gospels* in which were set forth miracles wrought by Jesus as a boy. The Christians insisted that the official acts of Pontius Pilate must have made reference to the crucifixion of Jesus; but as they had no access to any such report they produced forged Acts of Pilate.

But our evidence is by no means restricted to the multiplicity of apocryphal books produced by different Christian individuals and churches. And it is not good enough to say that all such activities were due to heretics and false teachers, like Marcion of Pontus who issued an adaption of the canonical Gospels. There was a great power struggle going on in the Church and bitter rivalry, and to gain ascendancy both for doctrine and authority the protagonists were prepared to go to any lengths.

Thus in the latter part of the second century we find Dionysius bishop of Corinth writing to Rome, "As the brethren desired me to write epistles, I did so, and these the apostles of the devil have filled with tares, exchanging some things and adding others, for whom there is a woe reserved.

It is not, therefore, a matter of wonder, if some have attempted to adulterate the sacred writings of the Lord, since they have attempted the same in other works that are not to be compared with these."

Among honoured epistles were those of the martyred Ignatius Bishop of Antioch at the beginning of the century. The available manuscripts show that the genuine texts were greatly amplified by some unknown Christian writer or writers. As to tampering with the Gospels I may cite how one sect which favoured vegetarianism and was opposed to animal sacrifices altered the words of Luke's Gospel, so that where Jesus tells his disciples, "I have greatly longed to eat this Passover (i.e. the sacrificial lamb) with you before I suffer" they put instead, "Have I at all desired to eat this flesh of the Passover with you?"

This brings me to the consideration of the New Testament. Let us take the Gospels first. I do not want to be too technical; but it is well-known to Christians scholars that these books are what the Germans call *Tendenzschriften*, books written with particular aims in view. The aims are various and their causes arise essentially from Christian circumstances of the time, subsequent to 70 A.D., when they were written, some local and others more general. While the Gospels incorporate recollections of actual events in the life of Jesus and of sayings of his, the descriptions are in many instances slanted and a great deal of the teaching attributed to Jesus is bogus. This was fully in keeping with the practices to which I have alluded. If it was considered necessary that Christians should hold certain views, these would be made more readily acceptable if they were credited to Jesus and his apostles.

Exhaustive study of the Gospels has made it quite certain that they contain many inventions and manipulations; but the appearance of this is sometimes softened by referring to certain elements as primary and to others as secondary. For example, when Jesus asks his disciples whom they believe he is, in Mark's Gospel Peter replies, "You are the Christ" (that is, the Messiah). This is primary. But in Matthew's Gospel Peter says, "You are the Christ the son of the living God." This is secondary, because Peter, a Jew, could not have spoken in this way. In the extremely theological Gospel of John the greater part of the teaching of Jesus is pure invention on the part of the author, who makes his hero utter his own sentiments in his own style. John flourished in the closing years of the Emperor Domitian, when this emperor insisted that he be addressed as "Our Lord and God

Domitian." So John makes the apostle Thomas hail Jesus as "My Lord and my God", again an expression for which no Jew would have been responsible.

Some of the bogus Gospel material is designed to be corrective. The early Christians were very troubled by the fact that they were suffering persecution and yet the Second Advent of Jesus had not materialised as expected. Accordingly, parables and sayings were put into the mouth of Jesus to convey that his return might be considerably delayed, but would come suddenly and unexpectedly, and that his followers should patiently endure to the end.

There was another aspect of the plight of the Christians, who after 70 A.D. were more non-Jewish than Jewish. Their assemblies were not licensed by the Romans, as were those of the Jews, in spite of the fact that the Jews had revolted against Roman oppression. To appease the authorities the Christian documents therefore stressed that the Jews rather than the Romans were responsible for the death of Jesus, and in the Acts of the Apostles Roman officials are represented as treating the Christians in a fair and kindly manner and often rescuing them from the Jews. The antisemitic falsifications in the New Testament have inspired Christian hostility to the Jews down the centuries and caused the death and torture of millions.

We have to look at the Gospels, then, as documents designed to accomplish certain objects, not the least of which was to adjust the story of Jesus to the changed conditions of Christians several decades later and to the progressively emerging new religion of Christianity. The ends were held to justify the means.

Must we, then, throw the Gospels overboard? Fortunately, not in their entirety. Deception would have been too transparent if the authors had not included numerous authentic things which had been handed down, such as sayings of Jesus which directly contradicted what the churches were teaching. For example, where Jesus urges his followers to observe the Laws of Moses, and where he announces that he was sent only to the lost sheep of the house of Israel. On linguistic grounds we can detect where he employs hebraic terms, idioms and constructions, alien to Greek usage. There are names of places, references to events, social and religious life and customs, geographical and historical circumstances, which someone unfamiliar with Palestine at the time of Jesus would be unlikely to know about. Occasionally we can see adaptation at work. When a paralytic was brought to Jesus and the bearers of the stricken man could not get through the crowd, Mark's Gospel tells how they went up on the flat roof of the house and dismantled part of it, evidently by breaking through the wattle and plaster. Luke's version, however, makes the men remove tiling, which for his Graeco-Roman readers would be the appropriate action.

The Gospel writers were not wicked men. They wanted to keep what they could from written and oral tradition. But they felt that certain necessities were laid upon them to influence those for whom they wrote by presenting Jesus and his message in a manner that answered to current requirements.

They did not regard their alterations and inventions as in the least culpable. But what they did has created a deal of trouble for those in quest of the historical Jesus, and has misled millions of sincere people who have believed that Jesus really did say all that he is credited with saying. Patient research, textual and historical, is progressively bringing us nearer to the truth. In this respect we should thankfully recognise that had it not been for the Evangelists with all their romancing and special pleading we would have been in a much less favourable position to recover reliable information than is practicable with the assistance of their records.

To evaluate the New Testament documents we have to relate them to circumstances affecting the Christians both from the inside and outside. The announcement that Jesus was the Messiah (the Christ) came at a time of crisis for the Jews when their land was under Roman domination and the people were awaiting a deliverer. Messianism for the Romans meant anti-Roman subversive activities. The Christians, by no means without justification, were held to be connected with a widespread underground conspiracy to overthrow the Roman Empire. They proclaimed another world ruler in place of Caesar, and announced that Rome was doomed to perish in flames. No wonder, then, when the Great Fire of Rome occurred in 64 A.D. the Christians were accused of carrying out their own predictions. Many of them were slaves or factious Greeks and Asiatics, who welcomed the promise of liberty in Christ and the creation of a new world order. When Roman arms triumphed, and the Jewish revolt in Palestine was suppressed, the Christians were under the necessity of disavowing any connection with the uprising, and is I have pointed out this demanded an anti-Jewish slant being given to the story of Jesus and the early Church.

But there were other effects. Before the war the seat of Christian government had been Jerusalem. Now there was a bid to transfer the centre to Rome. This could not be achieved without a great deal of falsification.

There could not be completely concealed what was well-known to many of the churches that there had been a steadily worsening rift between the Apostle Paul and the Apostles and Elders at Jerusalem headed by James the brother of Jesus.

The conflict had originated a long while back with the teaching of Paul, self-styled Apostle of the Gentiles, and had particularly to do with the terms on which he was admitting non-Jews to the status of Israelites if they believed in Jesus and abandoned idolatry. Paul insisted that these former Gentiles should not be required to become Jews by observation of the Laws of Moses. His teaching and actions were rejected by those who had followed Jesus in his lifetime and knew that he upheld the

Law. The bitter struggle which resulted is reflected on his side by Paul's letters to the Corinthians and Galatians. Since Peter also had personal contact with the Pauline churches as the approved envoy of the Christian Council, the names of Peter and Paul had come to represent the opposing factions.

An echo of the Apostolic position has reached us in a forged letter of Peter in which he is made to express his fears of what would happen.

"Some among the Gentiles," he writes, "have rejected my legal preaching, attaching themselves to certain lawless and trifling preaching of the man who is my enemy. And these things some have attempted while I am still alive, to transform my words by certain various interpretations, in order to the dissolution of the Law, as though I also myself were of such a mind, but did not freely proclaim it, which God forbid! For such a thing were to act in opposition to the Law of God which was spoken by Moses, and was borne witness to by our Lord in respect of its eternal continuance... But these men, professing I know not how, to know my mind, undertake to explain my words, which they have heard of me, more intelligently than I who spoke them, telling their catechumens that this is my meaning, which indeed I never thought of. But if, while I am still alive, they dare thus to misrepresent me, how much more will those who shall come after me dare to do so!"

What the new post-war Church Authority had therefore to do was to uncover a fraud, namely, that Peter had come over to the side of Paul. One of the documents concerned in the process was the revised version of early Church represented by the canonical Acts of the Apostles. This book is chiefly an account of the activities of Peter and Paul, with Peter preparing the way for Paul by admitting Gentiles into the Church, beginning with the Roman centurion Cornelius. At the famous Council of Jerusalem, when Paul was called to account for his conduct, Peter is made to speak out on Paul's behalf. We have only to compare Paul's Epistle to the Galatians with chapter xv of the Acts to see the transformation that has taken place. The book ends with Paul coming to Rome, the seat of the new Authority,

In Paul's letters from Rome, Ephesians, Philippians and Colossians, there is no hint of a reconciliation with Peter. If Peter did found the church at Rome, which is by no means certain, it is quite evident from Paul's statements that the church there in his time, 62 and 65 A.D., was intensely hostile to him, and when he was brought to trial no one would speak on his behalf. "At the first hearing of my defence no one supported me: everyone deserted me. May it not be counted against them!" Paul makes it very clear that the Christian community at Rome, largely wiped out in the Neronian persecution after the Great Fire of A.D.64, sided with the Apostles and Elders at Jerusalem.

The fiction of Petro-Pauline concord was concocted after both the apostles were dead, and in the period after the destruction of Jerusalem.

We have seen its influence in the Acts of the Apostles; but a further step was the composition of a forged letter of Peter, II Peter in the New Testament, where Peter is made to say, "Our dear brother Paul, according to the wisdom given him, has also written you to the same effect, as indeed is true of all his letters where he speaks of these matters, letters in which there are certain things by no means easy to understand, which the unskilled and unstable twist to their own ruination, as they do the rest of the Scriptures."

Pseudo-Peter is obviously writing at a time, decades after the real Peter's death, when Paul's letters had been collected and classed as Scripture, and by this time Paul has become Peter's dear brother.

The revived church at Rome, seat of the Imperial power, could only claim to have inherited succession to the destroyed church at Jerusalem by converting Peter and Paul into buddies, since these two were now widely regarded as the chief apostles. To this end the fraud was perpetrated and in due course gained ascendancy. For Clement of Rome, writing to the Corinthians about 90 A.D., Peter and Paul are "the good apostles" and he names no others. Less than a century later Irenaeus bishop of Lyons could declare that the true Christian faith had been handed down in that great, ancient and universally known church founded and established at Rome by the two most glorious apostles Peter and Paul, "and for this reason every other church and all the faithful everywhere ought to agree with that church."

I have now provided a number of examples illustrating early Christian fraud and forgery. But I should not neglect to mention Christian interpolations in Jewish books. A book greatly prized in the Church was one of the Jewish Pseudepigrapha known as *The Testaments of the Twelve Patriarchs*, the twelve sons of Jacob. The text as we have it contains a number of Christian additions to make the work refer not only to Christ but to the Apostle Paul. Paul was of the tribe of Benjamin, and therefore the Testament of Benjamin is made to speak of one of Benjamin's descendants "bursting in upon Israel for salvation and tearing away from them like a wolf, and giving to the synagogues of the Gentiles."

A more familiar example of such interpolation is found in the Antiquities of the Jews by the first century Jewish historian Flavius Josephus. This work circulated widely in the Roman Empire, and Christians found it very damaging to their cause that it contained no reference to Jesus. They therefore inserted in it a passage relating to Jesus in flattering terms, hailing him as the Christ and speaking of his resurrection.

We have to face the fact that the early Christians behaved in the same manner as their contemporaries in forging and falsifying documents, and that a great deal that is in the New Testament is the outcome of such activities, it means, I am afraid, that not a few elements in the Gospel story and much of the teaching of Jesus, including sayings which are highly prized, have to be treated as apocryphal. They illustrate the development of the Christian religion, but at the cost of misrepresenting its central figure.

As a kind of postscript I would like to add something about methods of detecting false material which bear on the New Testament. It is very easy to accuse investigators of retaining what suits their thinking and discarding what is inconvenient. Scholars of course disagree, but rarely do they pick and choose in an arbitrary manner. They are guided by criteria, notably by the progressively changing circumstances affecting the early Christians and the environment in which their teaching was produced, and also by the abundant evidence of Christianity's evolutionary development from an essentially Jewish messianic message to a quasi-pagan cultus.

T.E.Lawrence (*Lawrence of Arabia*) made the point in *The Seven Pillars of Wisdom*, when he wrote that "Christianity is a hybrid faith compounded of the Semitic as to its origin, and the non-Semitic as to its development.

It therefore carries within itself a problem, which as yet it is unwilling to resolve, and of which indeed it is not correctly aware... due to the extraordinary manner in which the Semitism in Christianity has been sublimated." Scholars have to try and avoid an approach which is conditioned by an attitude of mind. Several times, for instance, have I heard Christian clergy refer to the new teaching of Jesus to love your neighbour as yourself. They appeared not to be aware that Jesus was quoting from Leviticus in the Books of Moses.

Both the character of what is set down, and the idiom, can often determine whether we are in contact with early or late material. Jesus habitually employed a Semitic manner of speech, as would have been natural to him.

Where he does not do so we are bound to suspect the genuineness of what is attributed to him. Among other things to look out for are anachronisms.

These can be of many kinds, references to doctrines

which had not yet been formulated, institutions which did not at the time exist, conditions which had not then arisen. The New Testament and other early Christian literature offers many examples of deliberate and accidental anachronisms.

There are additional tests which can be applied to works credited to a particular author. Such tests have been employed, more recently with the aid of computers, to determine the authenticity of books standing in the names of some of the more prolific ancient Greek prose writers. One of the pioneers in this field has been Dr. W.C.Wake. The results have been most interesting. One of the tests is sentence length. The basis has been expressed thus: "We all write sentences of different lengths but the proportion of the different lengths is a habit which we keep for long periods and it is not affected by changes in subject matter." If a sentence length habit is established over a number of books by a particular author, and we find one or two which do not exhibit the habit there are strong grounds for suspicion that these are forgeries.

Another of such tests is the method and frequency of employment of certain commons words like the definite article, the verb "to be", and words like "and", "in" and "but". It is possible to establish an author's pattern.

Tests of both kinds have been thoroughly applied by the Rev. A.Q. Morton to the Pauline epistles in the New Testament. Of course there is the complication that Paul used amanuensis, whose own habits could make a difference.

But by and large the results are in line with other scholarly investigations, and we can place these epistles in three categories, Genuine, Less Certain, and False. The genuine epistles are Galatians, First and Second Corinthians, and Romans. The less certain are First Thessalonians, Ephesians, Philippians and Colossians, and First and Second Timothy. The false are Second Thessalonians and Titus. Philemon is probably genuine, but too short for test purposes. I would not like to commit myself to this verdict in its entirety, but I would agree that the first category represents what are the indisputable words of the apostle.

There is one more factor to which I must allude, and that is the changes which have been made in the texts by subsequent editors. Apart from the errors of copyists and attempts to standardise readings, we do have to allow for revisions and interpolations made in the interest of various schools of Christian belief. Even in modern times translations of the New Testament contain misleading renderings of the Greek.

The picture which I have had to paint for you is not a pleasing one. To some of you it may even be shocking that in the context of so much piety there should be so much turpitude. The knowledge should make us less dogmatic and more tolerant, and I would hope more ready to follow the Pauline recommendation to "prove all things; and hold fast that which is good."

(A Paper read at Eton College, Mar.4.'71)

The Legacy of the Essenes

The Claude Goldsmid Montefiore Lecture for 1992

Delivered by Hugh J. Schonfield, June 29th.

Rabbi Rayner, Ladies and Gentlemen,

The theme of my lecture is one which would have have had a special appeal to Claude Montefiore, and I deeply appreciate the honour of being invited to deliver it under the auspices of his name.

He was concerned to revive Prophetic Judaism, which he saw as a vital link between aspects of Rabbinical Judaism and aspects of Orthodox Christianity. He diligently sought for that link. He was anxious, as he once wrote, "to get at the facts, and to let them speak for themselves; to look at things as they really are." That was a laudable, but in the domain of religion, a somewhat difficult desire for he added: "That I shall seem to Jewish critics too Christian, and to Christian critics too Jewish is, I trust, likely, and is a source of some hope that now and then I may have said the truth."

I find myself this evening in much the same position, and if justification is needed I would plead that my researches have been conducted in the main in the capacity of historian, not of theologian. For most of the Christian Era the theologians have largely had it their own way. The objective study of history was not greatly in evidence, for it called for disciplines which were deemed secondary, notably those of literary and scientific analysis. For instance, one could take some Venerable work of religious instruction and treat it at face value, even accenting it as divinely inspired, whatever claims might be made in it or for it. But it could make all the difference to assessing its significance if one could ascertain where, when, by whom, and under what influences it had been composed. Further, comparison might be practicable with other texts, which could indicate borrowing or adaptation, ignorance of circumstances and contemporary conditions.

The historian's approach is very pertinent to our theme this evening, for we are considering a body of people of whom for many centuries all too little was known, and who were flourishing in the Near East roughly in the period from around 150 BCE to 100 CE. They are represented by the Essenes, or more accurately Essaeans, a term simply implying the Saints, successors of the Pious in Israel known as Chasidim. Certain authorities of the first century CE, who were their contemporaries, such as Flavius Josephus and Philo of Alexandria, usefully wrote about them, and there were some other references. It was conveyed that they were an eclectic Jewish society largely living in monastic communities—a major one being in the neighbourhood of the Dead Sea—highly esteemed for their piety, their prophetic gifts, and their medical skill.

Christian writers, notably in the fourth century, had been quick to see in what had been related of the Essene way of life, and some of their teaching, that there was a striking resemblance to the position of the earliest Christians. Sections of the Church had even preserved certain of their books.

The information taken as a whole was useful but somewhat slender, and there seemed little possibility a century ago that it would be greatly augmented. The Essenes hovered tantalisingly on the fringe of what was to become Jewish and Christian orthodoxy, and there was a mutual contentment of Church and Synagogue that they should remain so. Then archaeology stepped in.

But even before this some doubts had been creeping in that what these respective authorities had been desirous of depicting as Jewish life and thought at the beginning of the Christian Era had not, in fact, corresponded with the reality. This had not been a time when peaceful sages were instructing docile disciples in calm surroundings.

There were clear indications in the historical records that this period had been one of great emotional intensity, religious and political. Not only were the Jewish people in a state of revolt against an alien domination; they were moved and stirred by a religious obsession that the Last Times of the existing world order had been reached; that very shortly Divine judgement would fall upon all idolators and sinners, especially those in high places. Messianic personalities would appear both as leaders and martyrs in bringing about a transition from a world dominated by the Evil One, Belial and his minions, to an age of World Peace, Justice and plenty, in which the God of Israel would be worshipped by all mankind.

For such ideas to take hold of a nation, so that at a particular period they dominated and directed its actions to the point of total dedication and supreme sacrifice, there must have been authoritative pressures, pressures exerted by believed inspired writings. These had not come from the Schools of Hillel and Shammai, or from the moralising philosophy of the Hellenists. They could only have come from an impact which greatly transcended the influence of either the Pharisees or the Sadducees. Who was there who could have been credited with and have exercised such a powerful authority? There is only one possible answer. It must have been the Essenes.

But this seemingly obvious conclusion was played down by the theologians, first because it detracted from the interpretation they wished to furnish of the origins of their own concepts, whether Jewish or Christian, and second what had been handed down about the Essenes seemed largely to set them apart from the main stream of the life of the period. However, at long last in the Nineteenth Century things began to change. There was a widespread desire to acquire more exact knowledge of the antique past of mankind, and among the many applied sciences that of archaeology was enthusiastically embraced, notably what could be described as Biblical

Archaeology. In this context Egypt and Assyria were special favourites once their literature became accessible through the decipherment of their languages.

There was a less prominent, or perhaps less romantic and exciting side of these pursuits. This embraced the quest for ancient Biblical manuscripts, chiefly in the often uncatalogued libraries of various monasteries in the Near East. There were notable finds, such as the famous Codex Sinaiticus, now in the British Museum.

But it is not with these with which we are concerned this evening.

In the course of such pursuits there came to light a number of Jewish religious books of the immediately pre-Christian period. These did not belong to the Apocrypha attached to the Bible, and had been preserved in a variety of languages, Syrian, Slavonic, Ethiopian, Armenian, and so on. Some had previously been known by name, and even quoted: but now the complete texts were being made available at long last, not only to scholars, but also to the interested general reader. Certain of the documents had been interpolated by Christian hands, so that allusions in them could be made prophetic of Jesus.

The tone of these documents was morally elevated and largely of a prophetic nature. Because of what they professed to foretell they were described as Apocalyptic, and many of them also as Pseudepigraphic, because the authors had assumed the names and status of Biblical personalities, such as Shem, Enoch, Noah, Abraham, Moses, and so on. Scholars attributed these books to pious Jews of various persuasions.

What did not register at first, and indeed has not yet registered sufficiently, was that in the Holy Land immediately before the beginnings of Christianity there had been an outpouring of what must be called propagandist Jewish literature. Instead of this being a period rather barren of literary activity in Israel, as later orthodox Jewish and Christian sources wished it to be supposed, it had been extremely prolific and influential.

The books in question were filled with Messianic anticipations, and urges to lead a godly life because the end of the Ages was approaching. Nothing like this had happened before. When John the baptist and Jesus drew huge crowds when they proclaimed, "The time has come, and the Kingdom of Heaven is at hand!" they were not simply expressing their own personal opinions: they were echoing what had been prophetically announced by what they regarded as inspired sources.

Later on the early Rabbis did their utmost to suppress this literature, and to an extent they were abetted by the Church Fathers, because of the influence of such books. Both parties were anxious to convey that they did not subscribe to a militant Messianism, and had no design to overthrow the Roman Empire. Two disastrous wars with Rome had been more than enough.

The Tosephta to Jadaim (ii. 13) declares: "The Gilionim (Apocalypses) and books of the Sectaries do not defile the hands (are not to be treated as sacred). The books of Ben Sira and all books which have been written from that time onward do not defile the hands." The Tosephta on Shabbath (xiii.5) goes further and condemns all such writings to be burnt, even though there are references to God in them.

Leaving aside for the moment who were the so-called Sectaries, the historical situation as it existed in the first century of the Christian Era could not properly be assessed until the present century. The Jewish literature of the period, even as augmented by the end of the nineteenth century, still did not adequately explain the circumstances which the historian Josephus recorded, the overwhelming impact of Messianic notions, giving rise to violence and revolt, and producing such men as Judas of Galilee, John the Baptist, Jesus of Nazareth, and Simon Bar Cochba.

To get the past in correct perspective we needed much more information. But where was this to come from? It had not been anticipated that manuscripts from the time of the Second Temple could have survived in the climate of the Holy Land down to the present day. But before the modern discovery of the Dead Sea Scrolls there had been a portent.

In the Genizah of the old Karaite synagogue at Cairo Dr. S. Schechter found and removed a number of Hebrew documents. They included the book of Ben Sira to which I have referred. But I would particularly mention a previously unknown work, with parts of a second copy. The manuscripts were judged to date from the 10th and 11th century of our era. But the story they told was of a Jewish movement which had been pre-Christian in origin, and which had had as its leader a previously unfamiliar personality, described as the True Teacher, or Teacher of Righteousness.

Because of certain internal references the work was first ascribed to a pious priestly body identified as Zadokites. Its members had initially fled for refuge to the region of Damascus at a time when there was much Jewish apostasy. There, the Teacher concerned, acting as Lawgiver, had caused the faithful refugees to adhere to a New Covenant, as foretold by the Prophet Jeremiah. Thus later the book became known to students as the Damascus Document.

The information was exciting, and it was followed up, notably by Dr. R.H. Charles, a leading authority on the Jewish pseudepigraphic and associated literature. Investigation established that the recovered work had things in common with Karaite teaching. Now it had not been very long before the date of the Cairo manuscript that the Karaites had come greatly under the influence of those they called "The Sages of the Second Temple", whose writings had been recovered from caves in the Holy Land. The teachings of the Men of the Caves cherished by the Karaites had included reference to the True Teacher. It was to be deduced that the Cairo manuscripts were copies of one of these Cave documents, and much later this was to be confirmed.

What I am briefly relating took place before the first World War, and already then it was being suggested, notably by Harkavy, that the supposed Zadokites were none other than those we had known as Essenes. Another scholar G. Margoliouth linked them with the Primitive Christians, describing them as "the Sadducean Christians of Damascus."

More or less, there matters stood until 1947 when the great discovery of the Dead Sea Scrolls was made by bedouin in a cave near Qumran. Not long after, I visited this cave myself with the son of an Arab antique dealer of Jerusalem. But I did not stay long because of the great heat.

The first documentary spoils from the cave, as is well-known, were acquired initially partly by Dr. Sukenik on the Jewish side, and partly by Mar Athanasius Samuel on the Christian side. Some here may remember the excitement caused by the disclosure of the contents of some of the Scrolls, previously unknown and unheard of. Voices from the past had suddenly spoken, which called in question the veracity of aspects of the so-called Intertestamental Period which had passed muster hitherto.

Some scholars tried to defend the characteristic Jewish and Christian views, but they lamentably failed.

Further illumination came when it was remembered that there had been a letter preserved from the ninth century CE, which told how around the year 800 Jews had found in a cave near Jericho a hoard of Biblical and other manuscripts, and had conveyed them to Jerusalem. The letter had been written by Timotheus, Metropolitan of Seleucia.

So the remarkable modern discovery had not been the first. And it was now almost certain that the find referred to by Timotheus, which had included a collection of psalms, was the very same that had influenced and instructed the Karaites. And what was more, it appeared probable that some of the Apocryphal and Pseudepigraphic books recovered from monastic libraries had been translations of certain of the Hebrew scrolls into various languages.

I cannot sufficiently emphasize that we now had access to remains of what had evidently been a massive Jewish literature, for which those we had known as Essenes had largely been responsible. This literature not only belonged, in the main, to the century or so before the birth of Jesus: it had evidently at the time made a tremendous impact on the life and convictions of the Jewish people, who had long been deprived of the instructions of prophets.

In substance the Essene literature represented a new religious development, in which the words of the Biblical Prophets were linked with Iranian views of the age-old struggle between the forces of Good and Evil. The development had been one of the consequences of living under Persian rule. The outcome was a philosophy of the Messianic, which until then had never been systematically formulated. It employed methods of prediction which intimated that the climax of the Ages was fast approaching, that the Kingdom of God was at hand. The Jewish people living under the tyranny of Herod the Great and then Roman domination were increasingly stirred and excited.

Much that previously had seemed quite extraordinary became very much clearer with the aid of the new resources. We could follow more accurately the development of ideas as well as of events.

The Essenes had evidently stemmed from those known as Ghasidim. a body of pious Jews, many of them priests, who clung to the way of the Torah at the time, near the beginning of the 2nd century BCE, when the Hellenic way of life was becoming increasingly acceptable. A crisis arose when the Seleucid ruler Antiochus Epiphanes attempted to abolish Judaism, aided and abetted by certain of the high Priests.

Some of the Chasidim joined the resistance movement led by Judas Maccabaeus. After his death in battle others appear to have fled for refuge to the region of Damascus. There they were joined by an influential, but hitherto unknown personality, who himself had been persecuted by the apostatising chief priests. This individual is introduced to us in the Essene literature as priest, prophet and lawgiver, and commonly referred to as the True Teacher, or Teacher of Righteousness. It was he who caused the pious refugees to enter into a New Covenant for the observance of the Torah according to precepts which he laid down.

To his followers the True Teacher was indeed the Prophet like Moses, predicted in Deuteronomy (xviii.18-19). So Revered did he eventually become that the Essenes kept secret his real name, and under extreme torture by the Romans refused to curse him (Jos. Jewish War, II.152).

I have been able to discover indirect allusions to him under the names of Joseph and Asaph, both of them appropriate, the first because the Biblical Joseph was persecuted and banished, yet became the saviour of his brothers, while the Biblical Asaph was the author of a number of psalms. In the Collections of psalms among the Dead Sea Scrolls some appear to be autobiographical, and have been attributed to the Teacher himself. I may quote from one of these in Vermes' translation.

"Violent men have sought after my life because I have clung to Thy Covenant.

For they, assembly of deceit, and a horde of Satan, know not that my stand is maintained by Thee, and that in Thy mercy Thou wilt save my soul, since my steps proceed from Thee."

These psalms are very moving and illuminating as they tell of the Teacher's faith and experiences. The recovery of this great Jew from the Past, for so long forgotten and unknown, is a miracle for which we should be truly thankful. I wish there was time to tell you much more about him than I can this evening. But this would require a book. I have written one, but it is not yet published. I shall, however, be touching on one or two points. It is becoming increasingly evident, despite unawareness of his existence, how universally influential he has proven to be.

The True Teacher was to die in exile, but the legacy of ideas he left would in an extraordinary way be kept alive and influence millions. I have been able to trace some of that influence in Medieval Europe, and in the Far East in Afghanistan and Kashmir, where it became linked with aspects of Buddhism. Elements were transmitted by Islamic writers and Jewish Mystics, and by Christian monks of the Nestorian sect.

The task has been one of great difficulty involving years of research and pursuit of clues, and it was intensified by the two types of documents, one type which could be put into public circulation, and the other strictly for the instruction of their own initiates. The latter included also certain information about methods of interpretation, the use of codes and ciphers, and so on. As it has happened, through the find of Dead Sea Scrolls, we are now in possession of some books of both types, augmented by specimens previously available, chiefly belonging to the literature for external use. It is from the external texts that we get many of Pseudepigrapha, that is books written in the names of Biblical personalities, partly giving prophetic information and warnings, apparently from the past.

As an illustration I may quote the passage from a pre-Christian work, commonly known as the Assumption of Moses (i.16-18). Moses, shortly before his death, is giving instructions to Joshua, and says:

"Receive thou this writing that thou mayst know how to preserve the books which I shall deliver unto thee. And thou shalt set these in order and anoint them with oil of cedar and put them away in earthen vessels in the place which He (i.e. God) made from the beginning of the Creation of the World; that His Name should be called upon until the day of repentance in the visitation wherewith the Lord shall visit them in the consummation of the End of the Days"

Here is accounted for the availability of the Essene literature at the time when it should be required at the critical moment in history by the faithful in Israel, by putting the manuscripts in sealed jars and then hiding them away, the method employed with the Dead Sea Scrolls.

Many of the internal Essene books were explanatory commentaries on the books of the Bible, interpreting their words so as to make them prophetic of events and circumstances which were actually happening under the Seleucid rulers of Palestine in the 2nd century BCE and onwards, which had brought about the revolt of the Maccabees.

There were allusions to the True Teacher and his opposition to the crimes of the Wicked Priest, representative of the Hellenising High Priests of the time, the most noxious of whom was Alcimus, as we know from the Books of Maccabees.

Very rarely did the Essenes refer to individuals and groups by name. They used descriptive terms. Thus we read of the True Teacher, the Wicked Priest, the Scoffer, the Lien of Wrath, the Poor, and so on. This had the effect of avoiding giving a precise date to the circumstances related, since similar situations could arise more than once. Real persons and events acquired a relatively timeless significance as expressions of the circumstances in a cosmic drama involving the forces of good and evil.

The Essenes took themselves very seriously; but they also revelled in mystification, which fostered belief that they were much greater masters of secret lore and prophetic powers than they actually were. Thus they had grades of membership and individuals were initiated under the strictest rules and disciplines. They set great store by the significance of the letters of the alphabet and their numerical values, employing as means of interpretation and for the preservation of secrets a variety of codes and ciphers. They even inserted some into the text of the Hebrew Bible, probably when the books had to be reconstituted as a result of the struggle in the time of the Maccabees. During the Great Persecution by the Seleucid rulers quantities of Biblical manuscripts were destroyed in the attempt to suppress Judaism. In the second of the books called after the Maccabees in the Apocrypha the re-assembling of the sacred library is attributed to Judas Maccabaeus (II Macc. ii.14)

The work of maintenance was carried out by pious priests. So we read in the Essene book of Jubilees (XLV.16) how Jacob bequeathed all his books and the books of his fathers to his son Levi, "that he might preserve and renew them for his children unto this day."

One form of cipher favoured by the Essenes occurred several times in the Biblical book of the Prophet Jeremiah. The cipher exchanged the first eleven letters of the Hebrew alphabet for the last eleven, in reverse order. So Aleph was exchanged for Tov, Bet for Shin, and so on. The cipher was therefore given the name of Atbash.

The method was like substituting Z for A, Y for B, X for G, etc. To give an illustration: In Jeremiah XXV.26 there is reference to "the king of Sheshach."

By Atbash, Sheshach becomes Babel, Babylon. So the allusion is to the King of Babylon.

The Prophet Jeremiah was a significant person for the Essenes. It was he who had foretold that God would make a New Covenant with His people (Jer. XXXI.31-34). It was Jeremiah who gave instructions that the contracts for his purchase of a plot of land should be placed in an earthenware vessel "that they may continue many days" (in the manner of the Dead Sea Scrolls) as a sign from the Lord that "houses and fields and vineyards shall be possessed again in this land" (XXXII.6-15) It was Jeremiah again who proclaimed in the name of God a covenant guaranteeing that there would be always available a son of David to be king and a Levite to serve as priest (XXXIII. 1.26).

In II Maccabees, a book close to the Essenes, we read how Jeremiah before the overthrow of Jerusalem by the Chaldeans caused the Tabernacle, and the Ark of the Covenant, and the Altar of Incense, to be hidden away in a mountain cave. The Prophet then declared that "the place shall be unknown until God gather the people again together, and mercy come; and then shall the Lord disclose these things" (II.1-8). In the same work there is related a dream of Judas Maccabaeus in which Jeremiah appears to him and delivers to him a golden sword with these words: "Take this holy sword, a gift from God, wherewith thou shalt smite down the adversaries" (XV.11-16) It is worth noting that the mysterious title Maccabee in Hebrew converts by Atbash to Yad-Shem, the Hand of God.

The Essenes believed it to be part of their function to interpret the Bible prophetically in relation to the Last Days, employing such devices as I have indicated. The True Teacher is presented as the great Master in this respect.

The Essene Commentary on Habakkuk speaks of him as "the Priest whom God placed in the house of Judah to explain all the words of His servants the Prophets (and to expound) from the Book of God all that will befall His people Israel."

We have to see the Essenes as the architects of the Messianic. It was they who gave it a precision it had not had previously, and constructed what we now call Eschatology, a science of the Last Times.

The Essenes deduced from the intimations of the Bible that there must be two Messiahs, "anointed ones", one from the priestly tribe of Levi and one from the royal tribe of Judah. Of these the first would be the superior of the second, since the priesthood was more immediately the representative of God and directly engaged in His service. Necessarily the Priestly Messiah would be a person of exemplary character, a person of the type of the Patriarch Joseph in the Bible, who would suffer rather than sin. The Royal Messiah would be another David, a leader, but also a man of God ready at all costs to carry out His will. Thus from Levi and Judah would ultimately arise the salvation of Israel.

But almost in the shadows, in the background of these figures, and thus less defined, was the ultimate Prophet behind both Priest and King, anticipated to be the True Teacher returned or reincarnated. He was seen also as the Second Adam for the inauguration of the Redeemed World.

The fulfilment of these expectations; was first believed by some to have been achieved by the Maccabean rulers, especially by John Hyrcanus, who reigned in Israel from 134 to 104 BCE. He was hailed as prophet, priest and king, as Josephus reports (Jewish War, 1.68) The new dynasty of priest-kings had taken the title of "Priest of the Most High God", the title in Abraham's time of Melchizedek King of Salem(see Ps.cx)

Reference is made to these circumstances in the Testaments of the XII Patriarchs (Levi.viii.14-15). where we read: "A king shall arise in Judah, and shall establish a new priesthood... And his presence is beloved, as a prophet of the Most High."

But the Hasmonean dynasty soon gave Evidence that even the best of its members did not answer to the requirements of the Messianic concept. There was, therefore, seen a need to interpret it differently. The party of the Pharisees, which now came into prominence, adapted the Essene concept to suit their own views. The Pharisees, despite the patronage of Queen Alexandra (widow of the Hasmonean monarch Alexander Jannaeus), favoured a democratic rather than a hierarchic system. They now taught that there would be only one Messiah, of the line of David. But they could not eliminate the Priestly Messiah. They decided to substitute for him the person of the Prophet Elijah.

In the book of Malachi in the Bible the return of Elijah was predicted as an instrument of reconciliation before the coming of "the great and terrible Day of the Lord." The Pharisees built on this, and assigned to Elijah the role of forerunner of the David Messiah,

They got round the problem of the Priestly Messiah by claiming that Elijah had been a priest. He was so regarded by the Rabbis.

But while the Temple at Jerusalem stood the Essene doctrine of independent priestly and royal Messiahs persisted. So when John the Baptist, son of the priest Zechariah, began his activities, a great many of his followers hailed him both as the Messiah and True Prophet. After his execution by the Herodian ruler of Galilee, Herod Antipas, a sect of believers in him was established. They suffered persecution, and eventually emigrated, finishing up in Iraq, where the sect survives to this day under the name of Mandaeans, though the members actually call themselves Nazoreans.

Claims to be the royal Messiah, on the other hand, were made by and on behalf of Jesus of Nazareth, who was a descendant of King David. He also appears to have identified himself as the True Teacher of the Last Times, the incarnated Son of Man. The accounts given in the Gospels convey that his conception of the Messiahship was partly Essene and partly Pharisee. Thus he is represented as seeing in John the Baptist the fulfilment of a martyred Levitical figure, and also the returned Elijah. There are indications in the New Testament, especially in the Acts of the Apostles that after the death of Jesus, followed by his resurrection and temporary ascension to heaven, those who formed the first Christian communities were largely a combination of Essenes and Pharisees.

Pentecost, the chief festival of the Church, was also that of the Essenes, and its form of organization as described was also based on that of the Essenes, as now further illustrated by the Dead Sea Scrolls.

The discovery of the Essene documents no less explains why the Apostle Paul, as Saul the persecutor, should have hastened particularly to the region of Damascus to arrest members of the 'the Way' (an Essene term) who had fled from Judea. They could expect to find refuge with the Essenes who, as we now know, had much earlier established themselves in the same area.

That they would have been welcomed we may judge from a passage in one of the so-called Psalms of Solomon. "They that love the assemblies of the saints fled away from them (the evildoers in Jerusalem); and they flew like sparrows who fly from their nests; and they were wandering in the wilderness to save their souls from evils and precious in their eyes was the sojourning with them of any soul that was saved from them (the evildoers)" (Ps. XVIII, 17-19)

Saul abandoned his activities through seeing a vision, and then he spent three years on the borders of Nabatean Arabia, probably with one of the communities. He speaks in an autobiographical passage of the visions and revelations he had at that time (II. Cor. XII.) Certain it is that when we study his letters we find abundant evidence of Essene terms and teachings. Some no less correspond with the esoteric teachings of Judaism, a branch of study known as Maaseh Bereshith, the Mystical Lore of Creation based on the account in Genesis, especially where it is said that Adam was made in the image of God. Paul, like certain of the early Rabbis, believed that God had created a heavenly archetypal man, and the first man on earth was made in that likeness. This conviction derived from the Essenes.

The new evidences we have from the Scrolls are of assistance here; and what we can discover illustrates how wrong Christianity has been in its interpretation of Pauline doctrine. Paul never thought of Jesus as God, but as a fresh incarnation of the heavenly archetype of Man in the capacity of Messiah, to take away the curse of death inflicted on Adam when he sinned. The doctrine of the Trinity is nowhere in the New Testament, and largely based on ignorance of the sense of Paul's language.

But we also find in one book of the New Testament, the Epistle to the Hebrews, an attempt to claim for Jesus that he was himself both the Priestly and Regal Messiah, in spite of the fact that he was of the tribe of Judah, not Levi. The author insists, as was done by supporters of John Hyrcanus, that as King he was representative of the promised new priesthood "of the Most High God" after the order of Melchizedek.

A later Christian writer, Ephraim the Syrian, would have it that Jesus had been also of Levitical descent. He cites the account of Jesus having sent Peter to catch a fish in order to pay tribute, "and (and I quote) when he had drawn out the fish, which had in its mouth a stater, the symbol of dominion, those haughty ones (the Pharisees) were reproved and confounded, because they believed not that he was a Levite, to whom the sea and the fishes were witness that he is king and priest."

It is well known that the early Christians in their symbolism notably employed the sign of the fish. But it is not so well known that Essene tradition equated the Signs of the Zodiac with the names of the children of Jacob, and Pisces (the fish) was assigned to Levi.

It is of particular interest that we have this information in a Syriac work quoting a Greek author name Andronicus, who himself cited a Jewish authority called Asaph. Dr. A. Mingana, who edited the text, considered that Andronicus might be Andronicus Cyrrhestes, who died about 100 BCE, a noted astronomer credited with the setting up of the marble tower at Athens, now known as the Temple of the Winds.

If Mingana was correct this would date the mysterious Asaph no later than the 2nd century BCE. Now in the Assumption of Moses, which I have quoted earlier, there is reference to a Jewish zealot at the time of the Maccabean Revolt in that century, who bears the obviously disguised name of Tacho. Treating this as perhaps another case of the Essene use of the Atbash cipher, I was rewarded by discovering that Tacho turned into Asaph, one of the Biblical names employed by the Essenes in substitution for the real name of their founder the True Teacher.

Following up this clue I noted that a Hebrew medical treatise had been in circulation in the Middle Ages under the name Sepher Asaph or Sepher ha-Refuot. It attributed the origins of medicine to Shem, and the language of the work had things in common with expressions in the Dead Sea Scrolls. What was more it contained a form of covenant on lines offering a Jewish alternative to the Hippocratic Oath.

One of its clauses read: "You shall not mix a deadly drug for any man or woman, so that he or she should kill their fellow-man." The treatise was variously attributed to Asaph the Younger, Asaph the Sage, Asaph the Physician, and even Asaph ben Berechiah the Astronomer.

The Essenes, as is well-known, were noted for their medical skill and knowledge of drugs, and claimed that these arts had been handed down from the Patriarch Noah through his son Shem, and were transmitted eventually by Jacob to Levi, and finally reached the Essenes. Of course in earlier times down to comparatively recently medicine and astrology were associated arts, and it was fascinating to discover how Essene information had at least in part endured and was spread through Europe in the middle Ages.

From the viewpoint of religious teaching the Essene beliefs affected not only the Jewish Karaites, but also in Europe the Christian sect of Cathars who had links with the order of Knights Templar, whose ostensible function was to keep the ways open in the Holy Land for visiting pilgrims.

The contacts of the Templars brought them into association with Gnostic and Essene mysteries, so that they were said privately to deny the deity of Jesus. What was more they were accused of revering an idol in the form of the head of a bearded man which bore the name of Baphomet. Until now this has remained a puzzle. But I have been able to solve it by writing the word Baphomet in Hebrew Letters and treating it as another use of the Atbash cipher. The meaningless name then converted to Sophia which is the Greek for Wisdom. I cannot this evening go into details. But I may mention that the Archetypal man among the Essenes was represented in esoteric Judaism in the Kabbalah by a man's figure, in which the parts of the body bore the names of the 10 Sefiroth, or attributes of God. The bearded head represented Ghochmah, Wisdom.

There can now be little doubt that much Essene teaching and tradition spread both West and East in the Middle Ages. Partly this was due to the recovery of Dead Sea Scrolls at that time, of which I have spoken, and partly to contacts made by the Crusaders and the advance of Islam into southern Europe. I have instanced the Karaites and the Cathars among religious groups which drew upon the information spreading from the "Middle East".

One work which came into Europe at this time and was favoured by the Cathars was entitled Barlaam and Josaphat. This was a Christianised version of the life of the Buddha. A Hebrew version appeared in the thirteenth century under the title Ben Hamelech Vehanazir ("The Prince and the Dervish"). But the hero of the book was originally called not Josaphat but Yo-asaph, and proved to be linked with the Joseph-Asaph representation of the True Teacher of the Essenes.

There was discoverable that to an even greater extent Essene ideas had passed from land to land in the Far East. There were numerous references to a mysterious Yuz-asaph or Yus-asaph. He appeared as the travelling prophet robed in white, the Essene garment, who had come from the Middle East around the beginning of the Christian Era, and had finally settled in Kashmir where he died, and his tomb—a Jewish tomb—survives to this day at Srinagar.

In modern times attempts have been made to link the traditions with the person of Jesus, who, it is suggested, survived crucifixion and journeyed eastwards to preach to the lost Ten Tribes of Israel. Those tribes, according to tradition, gave rise to the Afghans. Curiously the legend survives that two sons of King Saul were named Barkhiya (Berechiach and Armijah (Jeremiah). Barkhiya was the father of Asaf, and Armijah begat Afghana. Thus the Afghans sprang from a nephew of Asaph son of Berechiah.

To follow up all the legends and traditions is a fascinating task, and I can only hope this evening to have whetted your appetite for further enlightenment.

What I may hope to have conveyed is that the Essenes have been of much greater consequence than has been believed hitherto. As an organized Jewish body they are no longer with us. But what they represented has never ceased to inform and inspire, and all the great Faiths of the world stand in their debt.

For much of the Essene legacy we are also in the debt of that Jewish prophet and visionary of the time of the Maccabees whose real name we may never know, and who now emerges from the hidden past as the True Teacher. I would like to conclude with his own words, from one of the psalms attributed to him, as translated by G. Vermes.

Always,
  at the genesis of every period
  and at the beginning of every age,
  and at the end of every season,
  according to the statute and signs,
  appointed to every dominion,
  by the certain law from the mouth of God,
  by the precept which is
  and shall be for ever and ever without end,

Without it nothing is nor shall be,
for the God of knowledge established it,
and there is no other beside Him.

The Divine Plan Of World Government

When a man is charged with making known divine counsels he has not so much to weigh his words as his own soul; and if he can feel that he comes to his task with faith and assurance he also approaches it with spiritual fear and concern—as I do now—lest he himself should be an obstacle to the acceptance of the message.

Most of us will have recognised that we have been brought together for a very dangerous purpose, to consult on the destruction of anarchy and its replacement by theocracy—the rule of God in the lives of men and nations. We are conspirators, and we are handling dynamite, not the feeble explosive of limited range and effectiveness, but the far more devastating force—the dunamis—the power of the Holy Spirit.

Let us think well before we touch off this terrible bomb of love and righteousness. It will probably cost us our lives: it will certainly transform them and change the face of the world. Are we prepared for the consequences of what we think to do? Are we willing for ties to be broken, for our measured existence to be shattered into a thousand fragments, for things we have called our own to be not our own, and for sorrows and sufferings which are endured by others to become our own?

If we are not ready for all this it is hardly God's peace on earth that we are seeking, but more the extension of a selfish tranquillity, the acquiescence in a common standard of tolerable iniquity.

I know what readiness means, and I am among you as one who reaches out in trust for the will to obedience. I desire to be made ready, and all of us at this Conference surely wish that what we have learned and what we have still to learn will strengthen and help us to overcome our natural shrinking from a grave and pressing responsibility. There are things which I have to say to you, strange and difficult things, which need that your minds and hearts should be open and attentive.

The message I bring is reinforced by the knowledge that both the time and occasion are opportune for its delivery; but I cannot conceal that it will involve us in definite action if we receive it, for its whole purport is to set forth the divine plan of world government.

Birth made me a member of that ancient people which first used the expression—the Kingdom of God—and gave to humanity the ideal of a society which would draw its inspiration direct from the Fountainhead of goodness and truth. Woven into the very fabric of the conception is the idea of holiness, the sanctification of all life and all ministrations as between man and God and between man and man. Nowhere in it is there room for pride or self-seeking.

But it is not enough to know the spiritual and historical implications of the Kingdom of God. We must know that we are in it, and of it, that we are one with the Initiator and Instigator of this regime. Those who went before us failed to establish the Kingdom of God because they could not bear to be different, to be dedicated. My own people first, and then the Church, broke their compact. When God appointed them to separateness, to be a nation apart, they would be like the other nations. They would have dominion and power and glory in its ignobler forms rather than yield up all such things to God to whom they supremely belong.

And what has been the result? That in this twentieth century we have a world stained with strife and hatred, and nowhere a refining and purifying influence to put a restraint on the worst passions of mankind.

I do not know what individually you believe the Kingdom of God to be, or how it is to be achieved; but those who have studied the Bible should at least be familiar with its essential features. Every age, however, has its own revelation, and there are still mysteries in the

Scriptures which in other ages were not made known, and which the Spirit of God declares at the due season when prevailing conditions make their application comprehensible. One of those epochs was reached nineteen hundred years ago: we have reached another now.

The gospel of the Kingdom of God for the coming era is the gospel of the holy nation. It is fully dealt with in the Bible, yet its full implications could not be understood until to-day. This is what I have called the divine plan of world government.

The plan emerged on the plane of history and commenced to become effectual with the call of Abraham the Hebrew, to whom God said: "I will make of thee a great nation... and in thee shall all families of the earth be blessed." In this promise is the first intimation of something different from the common conception of the function of nationhood, something far removed from the lust for conquest and tribal egoism. A nation is to come into being in which all others are to be blessed.

At that time God began to fashion a people to serve the very end for which the nations of our own time have been trying in vain to set up adequate machinery. The seer Balaam, looking down from the heights upon the tents of Israel in the wilderness, was inspired to proclaim:

> How shall I curse, whom God hath not cursed?
> Or how shall I defy, whom the Lord hath not defied? From the top of the rocks I see him,
> And from the hills I behold him:
> Lo, the people shall dwell alone.
> And shall not be reckoned among the nations.

—A people dwelling alone, not reckoned among the nations. It is for such a nation that the world has unwittingly been in quest, one which is separated from its problems of boundaries, and raw materials, and living-space, a nation that is international, intimately affected through its members by all the vicissitudes of states and yet so universal in outlook as to be capable of transcending the exclusiveness of more limited sovereignties.

To Israel God declared through Moses: "Now therefore, if ye will obey My voice indeed, and keep My covenant, then shall ye be unto Me a special possession from among all peoples—for all the earth is Mine—and ye shall be unto Me a kingdom of priests, and an holy nation." And again: "Ye shall be holy unto Me: for I the Lord am holy, and have severed you from other people, that ye should be Mine."

The imagination of a holy nation is so august, that it seems impossible to credit human genius with it, especially in the barbaric age in which it was made known. Yet there was much in the content of the conception that could only be illustrated when within the nation itself there existed a priestly tribe.

The economy of Israel in the wilderness now plainly appears as a microcosm, the priestly tribe of Levites performing the same function in Israel as Israel was to perform in the world of nations. It is written: "At that time the Lord separated the tribe of Levi... to stand before the Lord and to bless in His name.. Wherefore Levi hath no part nor inheritance with his brethren; the Lord is his inheritance according as the Lord thy God promised him." Just as Israel was to bless all nations so the Levites blessed the twelve tribes, and just as Israel was to dwell alone and not be reckoned among the nations so the Levites dwelt alone and were not reckoned among the tribes of Israel.

The description which the Pentateuch gives of the divinely ordained arrangement of the camp of Israel further makes it clear that we are looking at a scale-model of the larger economy. Central in the scheme is the Tabernacle of Meeting, God's dwelling place. Immediately about the Tabernacle are disposed the priestly tribe, while in groups to the north, south, east and west of it, are placed the tents of the twelve tribes. These positions signify the relation of the holy nation to the other nations, and enable us to understand the dark saying in the Song of Moses:

> When the Most High divided to the nations their inheritance,
> When He separated the sons of men,
> He set the bounds of the people
> According to the number of the children of Israel.

It is evident that the Pentateuch brings symbolically before us a plan of world government which has not so far been established, and differing from any that human genius has hitherto proposed. It is the plan of a theocracy-for God must be central in any enduring scheme—but in its operation it provides for the isolation and sanctification of one nation out of all nations through which justice and well-being can be assured to every people.

Among certain nations at the present time there is a vaunting of race often expressed in terms of a divine choice: its fruits are manifest in savagery and selfishness. This is a revival of the spirit of idolatrous imperialism, a counterfeit of God's intention, having every quality except that of righteousness and holiness. Let there be no misunderstanding to blind our minds to the fact that "God hath chosen the foolish things of the world to confound the wise; and God hath chosen the weak things of the world to   confound the things which are mighty; and base things of the world, and things which are despised hath God chosen." The function of the chosen people is one of disinterested service without self-commendation, and its supreme representative could truly say, "Blessed is he, whosoever shall not be offended in me." He also said: "Ye know that the princes of the Gentiles exercise dominion over them, and they that are great exercise authority upon them. But it shall not be so among you: but whosoever will be great among you, let him be your minister; and whosoever will be chief among you, let him be your servant." There could be no more explicit repudiation of domination and authoritarianism.

The choice of God undoubtedly carries with it an offence. That is why we have anti-Semitism and anti-Christianism. It is the offence of the cross, the instrument of degradation which has become the symbol of salvation. The status of the chosen people excludes boasting: it is not of works but of grace.

Israel of old broke the covenant of separateness and sanctification. But God's plan and purpose remained unaltered. Even while the people went astray the figure of an ideal Israelite, keeper of the covenant, was held before them. He, the Messiah, would be the glory of Israel and a light for the Gentiles, and Israel's mission would concentrate in his person. He would set the seal on God's new covenant with His people, whose law should then be written on their hearts and their iniquity would be forgiven.

I have no need to speak to this company of the life and works of Jesus, the promised Messiah or, as we say, Christ, except to point out that the most striking element in the development of the divine plan which he emphasised was that the accident of birth which made a man a racial son of Abraham did not make him a spiritual son. Physical descent could no longer be a sufficient qualification for membership of the holy nation. Many would achieve Israelite status who were not born of Jewish parents, and many born Jews would forfeit their status. The parable of the wicked husbandmen ends with the significant warning: "Therefore say I unto you, the Kingdom of God shall be taken from you, and given to a nation bringing forth the fruits thereof."

It is still a nation, and still Israel, through whom the divine purpose will be accomplished; but its constituent members will not all be of the same race. For Jesus the world remained a world of distinct nations, with the holy nation as its mentor and mediator. He taught the brotherhood of the faithful, which must precede the brotherhood of man.

How stood the chosen people after the advent of

Christ? The New Testament expressly condemns any theory of substitution, a casting away of Israel and its replacement by another people.

The apostles held and proclaimed that the Church is that very same Israel which was descended from Abraham, which was redeemed from Egypt, which received the law, and for which in the end Christ died. There was no break in the continuity of God's relations with His people; but there was a new forward impulse, a new building up, a new recruiting. And the larger number of those who were now included in the holy nation were formerly Gentiles. St. Paul writes much of the mystery which had been revealed, that in the new dispensation Gentiles could be fellow-heirs (with the natural Israel), "and of the same body, and partakers of God's promise in the Messiah by the Gospel." He tells these non-Jewish believers that they are Gentiles no longer, nor aliens from the commonwealth of Israel, nor strangers from the covenants of promise, for that the Messiah has broken down the barrier which in the Temple barred Gentiles from access to the Court of Israel. "If ye are Christ's," he says, "then are ye Abraham's seed."

St. Paul illustrates his argument, repeated in so many forms in his epistles, with the figure of the olive tree of Israel, from which some of the natural branches have been broken off through unbelief, and into which Gentile wild olive branches have been grafted through faith. These new Israelites are admonished not to boast of their acquired status, but to recognise its responsibilities, lest they in turn be cut off. On the other hand the day will come when with faith regained the broken off branches will be restored to their position, and so the holy nation will be complete.

It follows from this teaching, not only that all Christians are Israelites, but that all persons on becoming Christians cease to be Greek or Roman, French or German: they have "another king, one Jesus." The failure of the Church has been in large measure due to the refusal of its members to abandon their Gentile nationalities. It follows further that the future of the Church and the Jews is identical. They were ordained to be one and the same people, one fold and one shepherd, the priestly kingdom ministering to all other kingdoms, the holy nation sanctifying all other nations.

When the Church exchanged the status of a nation for that of a religion, and placed theology before theocracy, it inevitably postponed all prospect of establishing the Kingdom of God on earth.

Nearly two thousand years have gone by, and only now do the signs begin to appear of a turning back to the divine plan, and of a repentant desire by Christians to fulfil it. To bring about this change has required a social and political upheaval even more far-reaching than was effected in the ancient world before the advent of Christ, and an exile of Christians from the established churches greater than the exile of the Jews from the Holy Land. / External forces, the agents of God, have caused the emergence in the world itself of ideas of world community and world citizenship. It is seen by serious political thinkers that if peace and justice are to reign there must be a loyalty above that which is due from subjects to their own nation-state. Much is being done, and rightly, to encourage such ideas, but let us face up to the fact that the governmental union of nations is something very remote, and that it offers no immediate or even near solution to our problems. What we have to concern ourselves with is the bridge that will bring us safely to that farther shore.

In considering this bridge we must consider that the goal of our hope cannot be a new Babel, which apparently would satisfy many, a Cosmopolis in which all human viciousness would agglomerate: it must be a Theopolis, a City of God, into which shall be brought "the glory and honour of nations.". Into that city, we are taught, "there shall in no wise enter anything that defileth, neither whatsoever worketh abomination, or maketh a lie." The character of this goal should alone be sufficient to show us how far we are from it.

The bridge, then, must be one that will carry us eventually to the New Jerusalem, not to a New Babylon.

In the divine plan the bridge is called the Kingdom of God, and the builders of the bridge are the people of God. The international organisation above all others which has to be constituted and finally acknowledged in law is the holy nation, that into its fellowship may come all those who hear a call to world service and are ready to live according to its exacting standards. The functioning of such a nation is the only way in which the transition can be effected from world chaos to world order.

As one to whom the Gospel for the Nations has been committed, let me argue God's case with you.

If ever it was certain that the end of an age had come, it is certain now; for the world can hardly bear to contemplate its future. On every side there is thought of irretrievable loss, not of gain or of progress. We have reached one of a succession of historic epochs—the most critical of them all—when God must again intervene to demonstrate the way of life and salvation. 'If the end of the Mediterranean age required the advent of a Messiah, what does the end of this Atlanto-Pacific age require, but the coming of a Messianic Nation?

The redemptive agency this time must be a nation, because it is nations and peoples that stand in need of redemption. The emphasis is on the group and on the community. It is man-collective who is perishing, not man-individual. When men, as individuals, found themselves hopeless and lost, God sent a Man. Now He sends a Nation.

Before Christ came there had grown up an anticipatory belief in His coming, a belief which intensified as the advent moment drew near. We should expect similar evidences of the advent of a saviour-nation to be current to-day. Are these signs present? Assuredly they are.

It is difficult to take up any serious study of our perplexing world problems—whether in book, pamphlet, or article—without meeting again and again with the insistence on the necessity for an international authority. The League of Nations Union has made a slogan of it: "An International Authority is Essential to Lasting Peace." The question is posed with pathetic re-iteration, who can mediate and arbitrate between nations? Since the dawn of the century movements have been increasingly active which have as their object a unified system of control over the relations of states, and some have already been instrumental in setting up partially accepted machinery. We have a League of Nations, a Permanent Court of International Justice, and many lesser bodies and institutions. We have plans for Federal Union and the World Commonwealth. All of these endeavours stress the same heartfelt desire for a corporate power above and distinct from the nation-states, some authority that is supra-territorial and international.

Each articulate group has its own conception of the messianic authority, and how it is to function, just as the pre-Christian apocalyptic writers and prophets had their own idea of the Messiah, who he would be, and what he would do.

Neither does the comparison end there. Ecclesiastical students have seen how the Roman rule and Roman roads in the Mediterranean age made possible the journeys of the apostles who carried the Gospel message, while the widespread use of the Greek tongue made that message readily understood. If these and other circumstances had not existed the churches could not have been so quickly established throughout the world of ptolemaic geography. Everything was in readiness when the time for revelation came. Is it not so also to-day? Is not the world of global proportions prepared for the Gospel it is to receive? Space has been annihilated. Radio and cinema, telegraph and telephone, aeroplane, rail and steamship, the Press and the pamphlet, all now provide for the speedy dissemination of a world message and the creating of world organisations. Science, economics, culture and humanitarian enterprises, have been internationalised. "The interdependence of the modern world," says one writer, "means that a world order sooner or later is inevitable." We can see the force of truth in Madariaga's words: "The Divine will has chosen this our age for the world consciousness to emerge from the depths. Think what we will, wish what we may, we are all citizens of the world."

The anticipations of contemporary thinkers are still for the most part guesses at the kind of international authority which is feasible. Most of them take the long view to the world as it will become, rather than elaborate the process of becoming. It is God's Gospel that sets forth the process, that reveals that the authority for the transition era is to be a holy nation, as was foreshadowed in all the Scriptures. That nation is to arise out of the political amalgamation of Jews and Christians infused with the spirit of holiness. Together they are to fulfil the function allotted to them, the function of the chosen people.

We shall then expect that among the adherents of these theocratic faiths there will be evidences of a turning towards a corporate service for the world, an overstepping of the boundaries of religion into the territories of politics and economics. Again these things are so. Let me quote what representative Jews and Christians have been saying.

The Jewish author Leon Feuchtwanger has written: "I am bold enough to dream further than the most ardent Zionist, to dream that Jerusalem would become the centre not only of Judaism, but of the whole world. Yes, when I am quite bold, then I dream that Jerusalem might become for the world what the founders of the League of Nations had dreamed Geneva would become for all mankind."

Another writer declares: "We have done nothing as Jews for centuries. Cannot we be a conscious force making for nobler ends? Could we not, for instance, be the link of federation among the nations, acting everywhere in favour of peace? Could we not be the centres of new sociologic movements in each country?"

Here are two Christian statements. The first by Stanley Jones. "To those who are afraid of putting the Kingdom of God through the political order," he says, "we answer that there is no alternative. For if we do not control the political life with the Kingdom-of-God programme, then either Communism or Fascism will take it over."

The Bishop of Plymouth has pointed out that "It is only in view of the idea of a nation as a unit of service that Christianity can co-exist with a world of nations. To a Christian man, his duty to his nation can never be the first claim on his allegiance."

These statements, which could be multiplied, clearly exhibit the effort of an inner spirit struggling to break through the cramping walls of dogmatic religion into a larger sphere of activity and service for mankind. They begin to recognise a national function of an international character, and the sentiments are closely akin. Both for Jews and Christians, in fact, there is progressively manifested a conscious attempt at recapturing a status and a sense of mission which were taken for granted at the dawn of the previous Gospel age, but since fallen into abeyance.

What is now being recovered is the ancient Jewish universalism and the ancient Christian nationalism; for, for the purpose of the divine plan of world government, the chosen people must have a national and a universal aspect. The objective of an International Authority requires a community sufficiently independent to be an authority and sufficiently inter-dependent to be international. The revival on either side of the essential complementary characteristic points the way to the fusion of the two long separated parts; and the ground for amalgamation is the alignment that is taking place and the common conception of the Kingdom of God.

The revival of the theocratic principle of human government is indeed one of the major signs of the times. Stanley Jones is right in affirming: "As the demand for an all-comprehending principle and power for unity is now pressing upon the world-soul, this buried idea of the Kingdom of God is becoming a new, living issue. It is experiencing nothing less than a resurrection, and is becoming the question of questions."

Why is the existence of an international nation essential? Why is it preferable to have such a nation rather than any other institution for the settlement of world problems? These questions must receive an explicit answer.

We all know and appreciate the power of example and the influence of personal character. As Seneca has said: "Men trust rather to their eyes than to their ears; the effect of precepts is therefore slow and tedious, whilst that of examples is summary and effectual."

To hope to bring order into international chaos by moral persuasion, by high-sounding phrases of covenant and treaty, by declarations of rights and the passing of legislation, by pacts and pledges, if not entirely futile, is at least an expectation that depends for fulfilment on a long and laborious process for which, perhaps, there may be no opportunity. Neither men nor nations are readily made good by law. If it were otherwise the Covenant of the League and the Pact of Paris would have secured the world against war.

If Israel of old had kept the covenant, as they agreed to do, it would not have needed that the Messiah should come. But because they failed it did need that he should come in order to provide the example of an Israelite living in complete accordance with the divine will. We now know that man can be Godlike because Jesus was so, and the example of perfect manhood is held before us in Christ- likeness. Through the power of that example men have been changed.

It is the same with nations. If they could have kept the

covenant into which they entered, it would not have needed that there should be a messianic nation. But they having failed there must be demonstrated in a nation the ability to live up to international law. When one nation has shown what a people should be in all its relations, others will be transformed by that example. This theme is the burden of Sir Francis Younghusband's allegorical novel *The Coming Country*.

The thought of example, as applied to nations, is not foreign to contemporary political ideas. It is often suggested that Great Britain or the United States, as wealthy and influential powers, should "give a lead." Unfortunately, like the rich young ruler of the Gospel story, they are unequal to the demand, and hold back from messianic service because of their great possessions. Smaller groups of a non-national character have, however, responded to the call of discipleship, and there has been a notable increase in the practice of community-living. But because we are living in a world of nations no other kind of institution will satisfy the need for a national example. The Kingdom of God must be exhibited in operation in a nation before the rest of the world will be inclined to adopt it.

Another reason why we must have an international nation is to act as a bridge between the nation-state and the world-state. We are invited to begin to live and to think as world citizens; but those who are sincere in their advocacy of this nobility of outlook admit that its accomplishment is a rarity, and that at present the majority of people show little disposition towards such an enlargement of allegiance. The chill fact has to be faced that the world-state is to-day intangible and almost mythical. The nation-state is real to us: the world-state is unreal. We, therefore, have no sense of obligation to what is imaginary.

How then are we to proceed? Only by accepting God's plan which provides an institution at once national and international. There comes into being an actual nation with its own legal citizenship, which yet being supra-territorial with its citizens resident in every state is at the same time international., We have already seen that Jews and Christians are to compose this nation, the people of the Kingdom of God. The Jews present already the appearance of that nation in everything except legal nationality. The Christians are fast shaping to the same appearance, and by Christians we mean mainly those followers of Christ not of Jewish origin whether they are in the churches or outside them. The anonymous second century writer of the Epistle to Diognetus well described the Christian position as it once was and must be again. "For Christians," he says, "are not distinguished from the rest of mankind either in locality or in speech or in customs. For they dwell not somewhere in cities of their own... But while they dwell in the cities of Greeks and barbarians as the lot of each is cast... yet the constitution of their own citizenship, which they set forth, is marvellous, and confessedly contradicts expectation. They dwell in their own countries, but only as sojourners; they bear their share in all things as citizens, and they endure all hardships as strangers. Every foreign country is a fatherland to them, and every fatherland is foreign." This might well be a description of the Jewish people.

In modern language the rightful position of Jew and Christian in any country is that of a friendly alien. To regularise the position there is one clear further step to be taken, the discarding by legal process of all limited nationalities and the acquisition by legal process of a common extra-territorial nationality. Then you have immediately a true international nation, the bridge people that can carry the nations over to world union by a gradual transition. Membership of this nation becomes a real world citizenship, not an imaginary one, and it is a genuine national institution, which yet has no frontiers or racial and economic barriers.

The final argument lies in the desirability of detachment and for an uncompromising allegiance. There must be absolute dedication to world service and the theocratic mission.

Once more we must turn back to Christ for a precedent. It was necessary for Jesus to give up his family and city, while still loving both, in order to find mother and sisters and brothers among all who would do the will of God. He had to become the Son of Man. It is no less needful that the messianic nation, through its members, should surrender all other nationality, while loving the nation of their origin and place of residence, in order to associate with all nations and become the People of Man.

There are people to-day, among them pacifists, whose wider ideals conflict with the national policy. Their outlook invites the terrible epithet of traitor. Yet what are they to do? When we disagree with the policy of an institution to which we belong the honest and obvious thing to do is to resign our membership. But we cannot resign from the state, for statelessness is not a legally recognised status. We know something now of the position of the stateless person, and the temporary expedient of the Nansen passport. The only remedy is the creation of a legally recognised international nation. To this nation all who feel a call to world service can and should belong.

Something of the internationalism that is not directly subservient to state interests has already been realised by purely scientific bodies, by the International Red Cross, the International Labour Organisation, the Society of Friends, the Salvation Army, and other institutions. The bonds between the members of these bodies are cultural, humanitarian, social, or religious. All are in their way both spiritual and materialistic, and have won universal recognition and respect. For a like success in the domain of government it is required that the international institution should not only possess all these qualities, but should also be a nation.

The difficulties in the way of any other kind of institution are almost insuperable, and arise out of the very nature of their character. Madariaga, who for several years was on the League of Nations Secretariat, has stated that these difficulties are due to divided allegiance. "More deplorable," he writes, "indeed, almost unpardonable—is the sight of League of Nations experts, paid by League of Nations funds, trusted to give evidence as free and good men, who twist their advice to suit the policy of their own Governments. This spectacle can be witnessed again and again at Geneva." He claims that "the Secretariat should be, not an equitable and well-adjusted group of nationally-minded people, but a unit of world- minded officials."

That is the position, and the risk that is attached to every political organisation dealing with international affairs, whose members are not wholly divorced from their local nationalities. "No man can serve two masters," The judge, arbiter and mediator for nations must be utterly impartial, and not himself a party to the dispute. Only the international nation can assure a "unit of world-minded officials." What requires to be done is that this God-ordained, interpenetrative, disinterested people should as soon as practicable assume the status of a nation—and reign.

And if we ask, What title to nationality has a miscellaneous group of world-minded persons? we answer, The title in Christ to the inheritance of God's people Israel. The Jews have it by descent, the non-Jews by faith in Christ. In this, as in many other things, Jews and Christians are at one, and must unite. Our nationhood of a separate, priestly, world-ministering character has been provided. Nowhere will be found such another, neither is it in our power to create such ancestry or national corporateness by any artifice. Without our Israelite heritage we could be a religion, an alliance, a fellowship, but not a nation.

There is my case. I have shown you that God has a plan of government for His world, by means of which mankind is to achieve lasting happiness. I have shown the special need for the adoption of that plan in our own day, and I have indicated some of the circumstances which prove that at last man's will is approaching a confluence with God's will.

The plan is real and practical for the world which we know, though so many are still unaware that the God who made heaven, and earth and all things therein, is a greater realist than any of them. They imagine that what is spiritual is unpractical, though even academically omniscience must be infinitely more practical than partial perception. It is they, in their boldest and most elaborate schemes, who are pitifully unpractical; for their limitations render them easily liable to self-delusion, and there are essential considerations which they ignore and factors which they overlook. And because of this—

  The best laid schemes o' mice an' men
  Gang aft a-gley,
  And lea'e us naught but grief and pain
  For promised joy.

And so comes man trailing his failures a long way behind the "determinate counsel and foreknowledge of God," and reaching in the toil of thousands of years something approaching what the Divine Spirit had of old declared to be the system of government which alone can promote the world's lasting welfare.

But if mankind is slow of heart to believe what the prophets have said, it is an eloquent testimony to the intimate relationship subsisting between God and man that our sincere strivings do ultimately produce a kindred conception to that of revelation, because whether we are conscious of it or not God is after all working in us and through us.

So it is to-day, in our reaching out towards a uniting influence in the domain of international politics, that it is being suggested by some who would deny that they are thinking God's thoughts after Him that there should be created a legal international citizenship as a half-way step towards world citizenship. When we read such things we humbly welcome the inspiration, and thank

God for His compassion and grace manifested in His creatures.

Certain courses of action become constantly clearer. We know that whatever be the outcome of the conflict in which the nations are at present engaged the ensuing peace will be of no more than temporary duration unless we are prepared to become as little children, and to entrust to an adult authority for safekeeping some things that we are not trained as yet to use other than harmfully. We must hand over the matches and the pocket-knife to a "grown-up," and submit our national lives to a kindly discipline. But the "grown-up" must represent a wise and beneficent authority, and the discipline must be one which is loving and evokes love: we cannot surrender to an arbitrary authority much less to a potential bully.

We wait therefore, in the Bible words, with groaning and travail for the manifestation of the sons of God, for the holy supra-territorial nation to take shape and substance; for no other will serve our need. This does not relieve the world's governments from striving to better their relations in order that peace may be prolonged and equity prevail; because the post-war conditions will be terrible enough to require the aid of all men of goodwill to mitigate them. But it does mean that until the holy nation is recognised and recognisable many grave international problems must continue unsolved, and what is more fundamental the spirit that provokes war will remain in the world.

The prophet Isaiah described the holy nation as being born in a day; and if that day should not happen to be one of twenty-four hours in our reckoning it may still be expected to represent a remarkably short space of time. Spiritual births are normally more rapid than physical ones. Suddenly and stealthily, "like a thief in the night" as we are told, the Kingdom of God will be upon us, and no one will afterwards be able to declare the precise moment when it came.

The discovery by the world of a spiritual nation in its midst, wholly dedicated to its well-being in all spheres of human activity will provide the most dramatic episode in its fretful history.

Here at last will have been forged the true link joining nation to nation, a nation without frontiers and territorial possessions, inter-racial and theocratic, bringing under its aegis as time goes on all international machinery for the adjustment of differences and the promotion of cooperation, leading the world into the fruitful paths of order, peace and blessing.

The advantages of the plan, which is indeed God's plan, are obvious. Once trained on its objective the mind leaps to envisage all the fertile possibilities which it embraces. I know that there will quickly arise, there are now arising, those who will translate the thoughts into actions, who, fired by the Divine Spirit, will devote their service and substance as each is endowed to spreading this Gospel, to creating machinery and working out details, to assist in their own capacity great and small at the birth of a nation, the creation of which involves no dislocation or friction between states, which gives to them all and takes from none, and whose joyful fate it is to initiate the era of the restoration of all things.

Was There an Original Hebrew Gospel?

The quest for the historical Jesus has long been in progress; but since the creation of the State of Israel it has intensified. What more can we reliably learn of this distinguished Jew as an outcome? The answer to this question still very much depends on the study of the New Testament Gospels and how they originated.

Part of modern research, as represented by the Jerusalem School for the study of the synoptic Gospels (Matthew, Mark and Luke), has been directed to seeking an original Hebrew text behind these Gospels.

There was an article on the subject in the Jerusalem Post in the summer of 1985.

But was there ever such an underlying Hebrew text? The historian, as against the theologian, has to answer in the negative. And I write here as a Jewish historian who has devoted a lifetime to the subject, utilising all the resources available.

Certainly there was anciently a Hebrew Gospel in existence, known indeed as the Gospel of the Hebrews. In the fourth century a copy of it was in the Library at Caesarea created by Pamphilus, where it was seen and quoted from by Jerome. Around the same period the work was cited by Epiphanius, and a century earlier by Origen. It appears to have been attributed to Matthew. As yet, however, no manuscript of this Gospel has come to light. There is extant, however, a Jewish Gospel parody, the *Toldoth Yeshu*, and I have been able to show that that this was directed at the Nazarene Hebrew Gospel, and helps us to an extent to recover Its structure and content.

But the *Gospel of the Hebrews*, which has some value as regards the Jewish character of the teaching of Jesus as preserved by his Jewish followers, known as the Nazarenes and Ebionites, is in fact later than the Greek Matthew and was written in opposition to it. The surviving quotations show Jesus speaking very much as a Jewish teacher.

There never could have been a Hebrew Gospel underlying the Greek ones. The Synoptic Gospels are typical of the short biographies of the famous put out by Greek and Roman authors, for example the *Lives of the Caesars* by Suetonius. We have to turn away from the Gospels as biographies of Jesus to the original proclamation by his followers of the 'Good News' that in him the Messiah had come. Early Christian recollection states that when, in the first century CE, the Jewish apostles (envoys) went out from Israel into the Roman Empire with this Good News they carried with them two small documents in Hebrew.

One of these documents was a collection of Sayings of Jesus, like the Sayings of famous Rabbis. An early work of this type was found at Nag Hammadi in Egypt, and is known as the *Gospel of Thomas*. It does not have the biographical structure of the New Testament Gospels, and in fact Jesus advises his followers to rally round his brother Jacob (James) as their new leader.

The other document, said to have been compiled by the Apostle Matthew, was a collection of passages from the Hebrew Bible stated to have had their prophetic fulfilment in the activities of Jesus, and thus demonstrated his Messiahship. The Apostle Paul made use of this document, as later did Justin Martyr in his *Dialogue with the Jew Trypho*, though in an expanded form. Another writer, Papias, speaks of it as the work of Matthew, who compiled the Old Testament texts (said to predict the activities of Jesus as Messiah), "and everyone expounded them as he was able". Canonical Matthew employs such a source, which gave this Gospel its name.

But these two documents, valuable as they were for the purposes of the Gospel writers, were insufficient for a biographical record, a life of Jesus. For this an additional source was essential. And here again ancient information puts us on the right track.

The man who had been most closely associated with Jesus throughout his brief career was the Apostle Peter (Simon Kephas). According to early record Peter had visited the Christian communities of the Roman Empire, and wherever he went he related what he could recall of the Master's activities from personal experience. Peter spoke not in Greek, or even in Hebrew: he spoke In the Galilean dialect of Aramaic, and had with him an interpreter. This was a young man called Mark, who later made a collection of what he could recall of Peter's statements. This collection was the foundation of the New Testament Gospel of Mark, which though it is in Greek sometimes quotes words of Jesus in Aramaic, as Peter had uttered them.

Mark is the oldest of the Gospels, and notably contains no Nativity legends. It begins with the preaching of John the Baptist. A fact of importance is that the end of this Gospel is missing. It breaks off in the middle of a sentence. Whether this was due to chance or to intention we do not know. Was there something the later Church did not like? At any rate a new ending was substituted.

None of the New Testament Gospels was written in Israel or before the destruction of Jerusalem in 70 CE.

Matthew's Gospel employed Mark, and also the other two documents I have mentioned, one of which was in the name of Matthew. It originated in Egypt, where there was considerable anti-semitism. This is why this Gospel has attacks on the Jews, especially as regards the crucifixion of Jesus, and why uniquely it makes Jesus to have been taken to Egypt in infancy.

Luke's Gospel is later than Mark and Matthew, written almost at the end of the first century CE. It is the most literary and entertaining of the Gospels, and represents Part One of a Two Part work, The second is known as the Acts of the Apostles. The author acknowledges that many others before him had written an account of Jesus. He was not a Jew, though very sympathetic to Judaism. In the manner of many historians of his time he was not above inventing incidents to fill out his story, mainly taken from the Old Testament. He was inspired by the works of the Jewish historian Josephus, who had gone over to the Romans, especially his work Against Apion. This was in two parts also, and dedicated to a patron "the most excellent Epaphroditus". Luke addresses his own two-part composition to "the most excellent Theophilus".

The fourth New Testament Gospel, attributed to John, is quite unlike the others, and in point of time is the latest, around the beginning of the second century. It emanates from Ephesus in Asia Minor, and represents the work of two persons called John, neither of whom was one of the Apostles of Jesus. According to tradition the first John (known as the Beloved Disciple of Jesus) had been a Jewish priest of Jerusalem, in whose home Jesus had celebrated the Passover Seder before his arrest. At the time of the Jewish war with the Romans he had fled to Ephesus. He lived to a very great age, and was asked by local Christians to dictate his memoirs of Jesus. These came into the hands of a young Greek Christian named John who made them the basis of his own peculiar doctrine, which was strongly pagan. The very un-Jewish and anti-Jewish speeches of Jesus in this Gospel, where Jesus is made to speak to the Jews of "your Law", are the composition of the Greek John, as also the long address of Jesus to his disciples after the Last Supper. The tombs of both Johns were still shown at Ephesus In the fourth century.

The letters of the second John in the New Testament, as also an opposition movement to his doctrine known as the Alogi, shows how singular his position was at the time. Later, however, these imaginary speeches of Jesus became very acceptable to orthodox Christianity, and have remained so. But we can detect their Invention from their style. Jesus speaks in the manner that the author of the Letters of John in the New Testament writes.

There is always the hope that by good fortune Hebrew or Aramaic documents relating to Jesus may one day be recovered in Israel. Meanwhile there is still much to be learned from the existing sources, provided we employ historical methods of research, and are not restricted by religious inhibitions.

The Rod that Budded

A Springtime Reverie by Hugh J. Schonfield

When individual behaviour violates social order it is an established principle of a law-conscious community to seek a motive for the errancy; for it is held that it cannot be causeless and is unlikely to be without object and design. So too it has been considered irrational to regard History as a meaningless succession of events overtaking an aimless progression of human groups. Somewhere must be an explanation that will reveal a purpose; for there is every indication in Nature of the operation of law.

Once again we greet the recurring marvel of springtime, and we are reminded that for many thousands of years Man has been a close observer of the alternation of the Seasons, of the surging up of new life out of evident death, of the process of blossom and bud and fruit. We know that this rhythm begat his own faith and confidence, and quickened and informed the religious instinct which urged that he too had his destined fulfilment.

Dependent on the yearly miracle for sustenance primitive peoples symbolised the processes in their rituals in the childlike belief that they could lend Nature a helping hand; but out of this intimate association there emerged the dawning perception that the drama afforded a clue to the riddle of Man's own existence. Man discovered later that he could indeed assist Nature, that he possessed the creative ability of cultivation by which he could select, improve and perfect species. Gradually he began to react to this knowledge by applying its lessons to himself, by considering how he could improve his own kind by the cultivation of moral virtues. The qualities were defined which dis distinguished the good man. And might he not go further and eventually produce out of his own race the progenitor of a more perfect humanity? But in the case of the animal and vegetable kingdoms it had been a higher than they—Man himself—who had interposed his power to bring about their development and elevation. Would it not require, therefore, a higher than Man—God —to interpose His Power to aid the institution of a more perfect manhood?

And so there arose among the Israelites—a people of settled cultivators—the conjoint faith in a Divine purpose behind Man's creation, His selection of a species—the Holy Nation—and the messianic expectation of the coming of the God-endowed man out of their midst through whom the ultimate ideal order would be initiated.

It seems quite natural and appropriate that this faith should be linked with springtime. The selection of the Holy Nation out of all the tribes of men was symbolised in miniature by the calling out of the Levitic tribe from among the others. The heads of each tribe were bidden to take a rod to be laid up before the Lord in the tabernacle of witness. "And it came to pass, that on the morrow Moses went into the tabernacle of witness; and, behold, the rod of Aaron for the house of Levi was budded, and brought forth buds, and bloomed blossoms, and yielded almonds." (Am. xviii. 8.)

The advent in Israel of the God- endowed Man (the Christ) is likewise prophesied in terms of spring. "And there shall come forth a shoot out of the stem of Jesse, and a branch shall grow out of his roots: and the spirit of the Lord shall rest upon him, the spirit of wisdom and understanding, the spirit of counsel and might, the spirit of knowledge and of the fear of the Lord... and righteousness shall be the girdle of his loins, and faithfulness the girdle of his reins" (Isa. xi. 1-5). With him would begin the era of peace, the new sowing of the tested seed of the Holy Nation, imbued with his spirit. "He shall cause them that come of Jacob to take root: Israel shall blossom and bud, and fill the face of the world with fruit" (Isa. xxvii. 6).

Thus, according to this faith, there comes to be carried

out in History the work of the Supreme Planner and Cultivator, whose "field is the world."

It is this assurance which is our inheritance, and enables us to apprehend as a scientific proposition the inevitable emergence of the Holy Nation—the Christ-group of men—as the purposefully calculated result of the Divine experiment, which portends a new springtide for all humanity. With awe and joy we feel the sap of that spring rising within us to give us strength for our mighty task, and perceive the inner meaning of...

What lightens in the lucid east
Of rising worlds by yonder wood.
Long sleeps the summer in the seed;
Run out your measured arcs, and lead
The closing cycle rich in good.

Alfred, Lord Tennyson.